USING
GAMES &
SIMULATIONS
in the CLASSROOM

USING
GAMES &
SIMULATIONS
in the CLASSROOM

Henry Ellington
Monica Gordon
Joannie Fowlie

**KOGAN
PAGE**

YOURS TO HAVE AND TO HOLD
BUT NOT TO COPY

First published in 1998

Apart from any fair dealing for the purposes of research or private study, or criticism or review, as permitted under the Copyright, Designs and Patents Act 1988, this publication may only be reproduced, stored or transmitted, in any form or by any means, with prior permission in writing of the publishers, or in the case of reprographic reproduction, in accordance with the terms and licences issued by the Copyright Licensing Agency. Enquiries concerning reproduction outside those terms should be sent to the publishers at the undermentioned address:

Kogan Page Limited
120 Pentonville Road
London N1 9JN

© Henry Ellington, Monica Gordon and Joannie Fowlie 1998
The right of Henry Ellington, Monica Gordon and Joannie Fowlie to be identified as the authors of this work has been asserted by them in accordance with the Copyright, Designs and Patents Act 1988.

British Library Cataloguing in Publication Data
A CIP record for this book is available from the British Library.
ISBN 0 7494 2566 0

Typeset by BookEns Ltd, Royston, Herts.
Printed and bound in Great Britain by
Biddles Ltd, Guildford and King's Lynn

*This book is dedicated to our long-suffering spouses – Lindsay,
Fred and Donald – without whose help, support and encouragement
it could never have been written.*

Contents

Acknowledgements

We would also like to acknowledge the help received from the following individuals and organizations.

All our colleagues who provided case study materials, especially Eric Addinall, Bernard Brown, Hilda Creighton, Shirley Earl, Elizabeth Macleod, Linda Mudie, Fred Percival, Norman Reid and Alison Robb. All the various bodies who allowed their materials to be used, especially the Association for Science Education, Glasgow University, the former Grampian Education Authority, HS Software, the Institution of Electrical Engineers, Phillips Petroleum, The Robert Gordon University and the Scottish Education Department. Bill Black, for helping to produce many of the graphic materials and taking the photographs. Doreen Alexander, for processing the manuscript, as well as many of the packages described in the book.

Introduction

This book has been written by teachers for teachers. It is not yet another learned treatise on the theory of games and simulations, designed to be read mainly by academics and by educational research students. Rather, it is a practical guide to the use of games and simulations in the classroom. All three of the authors have made extensive use of games and simulations in their own teaching, and all three are totally convinced of the power, versatility and effectiveness of the approach. In this book, they show how other teachers can make equally effective use of games and simulations with their pupils – at all levels from nursery to upper-secondary and beyond. All types of games and simulations are covered, including card games, board games, role-playing simulations and computer-based exercises.

The history of educational gaming and simulation

Games have been played for amusement for thousands of years, and simulations (in their broadest sense) have an equally long history. The application of gaming and simulation techniques to education and training is, however, a comparatively recent development. The first field in which such applications took place was military training, where serious use of simulation and gaming began at the end of the eighteenth century. War games and simulations have since been developed to a high level of realism and sophistication, and all nations now make regular use of such exercises in the training of their armed forces.

The next field in which important developments took place was business management training, where the use of games, simulations and case studies as vehicles for developing decision-making and problem-solving skills was introduced in the mid-1950s. Here, there was a need to find a teaching method that could bridge the gap between formal academic instruction (which often lacked direct job relevance) and on-the-job training (which could be slow, and was generally restricted to a specific area). Around 1955, it was recognized that gaming and simulation methods could help provide a solution and, in 1956, the American Management Association produced the first business game. Led by the Harvard Business School, which made the 'case-study method' one of the mainstays of its teaching, the use of such exercises soon spread to business schools throughout the world.

It was not until the early 1960s, however, that the use of games and simulations spread to the various mainstream branches of education, with the initial developments taking place in teacher training and in the teaching of the social sciences. Although most of the early educational developments were again of American origin, educational games and simulations started to be produced in Europe in the mid-to-late 1960s – mainly for use in the teaching of social sciences such as geography, international relations and urban development. During the 1970s, however, gaming and simulation techniques spread to an ever-increasing range of other disciplines, including the various branches of science and technology. They are now used in the teaching of virtually every subject – and at all levels of education from nursery schools to universities. Indeed, they have proved to be one of the great success stories of educational technology during the last quarter of the twentieth century.

How the authors have been involved in such developments

All three of the authors of this book have been heavily involved in the development, use and promotion of educational games and simulations. The first to do so was Monica Gordon, who began work as a primary teacher in 1965 and immediately recognized the great potential of games and simulations as vehicles for enhancing her pupils' learning experience. At the time, primary teaching in Scotland was highly traditional, with the main emphasis being on the 'three R's', and whole-class teaching being the dominant mode of instruction. Monica soon started to develop classroom games and simulations to reinforce her direct teaching, to bring 'fun' into her classroom, to encourage self-discipline and group interaction, and to facilitate learning in new and different formats. During her subsequent 30-year career as a teacher, in which she worked at all levels of nursery and primary education, she continued to promote the use of such exercises and gained a national reputation as a curricular innovator. Latterly, her main work was at lower-primary and nursery level and, while she was Head Teacher at Aberdeen's York Street Nursery School, she played a key role in the 1990–91 Grampian Primary Industry Project – a major curriculum-development project in which teachers used games and simulations to help their pupils to learn about the 'business' side of industry. She retired in 1996, and now works as a consultant in early education.

Henry Ellington studied physics at university, and worked as a research scientist, secondary school teacher and physics lecturer before becoming Head of the Educational Technology Unit at Robert Gordon's Institute of Technology, Aberdeen in 1973 (the Institute did not become The Robert Gordon University until 1992). He immediately became involved in the development of educational games and simulations based on science and technology, heading a team that gained an international reputation in the field. He and his colleagues have now produced over 70 such exercises, many of which have been used in schools, colleges and universities throughout the world. He has been involved in promoting the use of games and simulations at all levels of education, and has played a leading role in several major curriculum development projects, both at national level (with bodies such as the Scottish Education Department and the Association for Science Education) and at local level (mainly with Grampian Education Authority). He was one of the organizers of the Grampian Primary Industry Project, during which he worked closely with the other two authors of this book. His many publications on the educational use of games and simulations include three books, *Games and Simulations in Science Education*, *A Handbook of Game Design* and *Case Studies in Game Design* (see Further Reading). He still works at The Robert Gordon University, where he is Head of the Centre for Learning and Assessment.

Joannie Fowlie was a comparative latecomer to the use of educational games and simulations. She started teaching in 1967, working at all stages of primary education and latterly concentrating on the upper stages (P6–7; age 10–12). It was while working as a P7 class teacher at Anderson's Primary School in Forres that she was nominated by her Head Teacher to take part in the 1990–91 Grampian Primary Industry Project. Although initially some-what sceptical about the educational value of games and simulations, she soon became an enthusiastic convert once she realized just how useful and effective they could be. Indeed, she subsequently agreed to be seconded to Grampian Education Authority's Teachers' Resource Centre in order to promote the even wider use of games and simulations throughout Grampian schools. During this secondment, she and Henry Ellington developed a 'do-it-yourself' kit for teachers on the design and use of classroom games, *A Guide to Games and Simulations as a Context for Learning* (see Further Reading). This was distributed to all 320 of Grampian's primary and secondary schools, and helped to bring about a very significant increase in the use of such exercises. Joannie has since returned to classroom teaching, and is currently Assistant Head as Head of Junior Department at St Margaret's School for Girls, Aberdeen, where she continues to use educational games as a learning tool for her pupils.

The purpose and structure of this book

This is very much a practical book, written with the needs of practising classroom teachers and teacher-trainers in mind. It should prove extremely useful to school teachers at all levels – nursery (age 3–5), primary (age 5–12) and secondary (age 12–18). Indeed, much of the content should also be of interest to people teaching the early stages of post-school education. Throughout the book, extensive use is made of illustrative case studies, which look in detail at actual games and simulations of proven pedigree and of ways in which such exercises have been built into the school curriculum.

The first three chapters set the scene by taking a general look at educational games and simulations. Chapter 1 provides some basic definitions, and then takes readers on a 'guided tour' of the game/simulation/case-study field. It shows how such exercises can be classified both by *function* (ie, in terms of how they are used) and by *format* (ie, in terms of the medium in which they are presented). Chapter 2 then examines some of the general educational characteristics of such exercises, highlighting their main strengths and weaknesses and reviewing some of the most important educational contexts in which they can be used. Chapter 3 then provides some basic guidelines on how to choose and use games and simulations. It also includes all the materials needed to run one particular exercise – *North Sea Auction* – with a class.

The next four chapters form the heart of the book, providing detailed guidance on how to use games and simulations with pupils of different ages. Chapter 4 deals with their use at nursery level, ie with pre-school pupils of age roughly 3–5 who have yet to acquire basic literacy and numeracy. Chapter 5 looks at how they can be used at early-primary level, ie with pupils aged roughly 5–8 who are still in the process of acquiring basic literacy and numeracy. Chapter 6 then covers their use at upper-primary and lower-secondary levels, ie with pupils aged roughly 8–14 who have (in most cases) acquired basic literacy and numeracy and are having their knowledge, skills and experience extended via a largely cross-disciplinary curriculum. Finally, Chapter 7 shows how games and simulations can be used with older secondary pupils aged roughly 14–18, where the curriculum is largely subject-centred and increasingly specialized. In each case, the authors review the basic characteristics of the stage of education being considered and examine the different ways in which games and simulations can contribute to the support and enhancement of the educational process. Each chapter ends with a detailed case study on how such exercises have been built into a major part of the curriculum in a particular school.

The final three chapters offer practical advice on how to design games and simulations for classroom use. Chapter 8 deals with the 'top-down' or 'algorithmic' approach to game design that is advocated in most books on the subject. It shows how it is possible to develop an exercise capable of achieving specific educational objectives with a particular target group by working systematically through a series of well-defined stages. Chapter 9 then deals with the 'bottom-up' or 'inspirational' approach that tends to be adopted by people who are unfamiliar with the algorithmic approach to game design. It shows how it is possible to develop perfectly respectable classroom games simply by looking at the range of games children play in their homes and seeing if any of these might be adapted for educational use. Finally, Chapter 10 looks at the additional educational advantages that can be gained by involving pupils in the design of classroom games and simulations, examining specific case studies drawn from the authors' own experience.

Three reference sections have been included at the end of the book in order to enhance its usefulness to readers. The first is a further reading section that lists books and journals related to the educational use of games and simulations. The second provides information about where readers can obtain those games and simulations described in the book that have actually been published. The third is a comprehensive index.

Although much of the material contained in the book is based on the authors' work within the British educational system, the treatment is sufficiently general and generic to make the book equally useful to teachers in all parts of the English-speaking world, particularly America, Canada, Australia, New Zealand and South Africa. Indeed, it should also prove useful in countries such as Malaysia and Singapore where English is not the main language but where most teachers are familiar with English. The authors hope that their fellow teachers will find the book useful, and will be glad to hear from anyone who is encouraged to use games and simulations with their pupils as a result of reading it.

1

A Guided Tour of the Game/ Simulation/Case-Study Field

Since some readers are probably unfamiliar with educational games and simulations, we will begin by defining a few basic terms and taking you on a short 'guided tour' of the game/simulation/case-study field.

Some basic definitions

Let us begin by explaining what educationalists understand by the term *game*. Here, most people accept the broad definition given by Clark Abt in 1968: 'any contest (*play*) among adversaries (*players*) operating under constraints (*rules*) for an objective (*winning, victory or pay-off*)'. Thus, to qualify as a 'game', an exercise must have two basic characteristics, namely, *overt competition* of some sort, and *rules* (arbitrary constraints within which the players have to operate).

One possible weakness of this definition is that it appears to exclude from the class of 'games' exercises in which *a single player* competes directly against the game system (patience, pinball, crosswords, arcade games, computer games, and so on). This anomaly can easily be resolved, however, by regarding the deviser of the game system as one of the 'adversaries' in such cases. Somewhat more disturbingly, it could also be argued that the definition includes most modern wars, since these undoubtedly incorporate 'competition', and are – in theory at any rate – fought under the 'rules' of the Geneva Convention!

Let us now explain what is meant by a *simulation*. Here, the generally accepted definition is that given by Guetzkow in 1963: 'an operating representation of central features of reality'. Thus, to qualify as a 'simulation', an exercise must again have two essential features, namely, it must represent a *real situation* of some sort, and must be *ongoing*, ie dynamic.

Again, the definition has a possible weakness in that it appears to exclude from the class of 'simulations' exercises such as *'Space Invaders'* and *'Dungeons and Dragons'* which are based on purely imaginary scenarios. This anomaly can be overcome by extending the definition of 'reality' to include all situations that could conceivably be real. It should also be noted that the definition excludes purely static analogues such as maps, plans and circuit diagrams, but includes working models and animated representations of all types.

Finally, let us explain what is meant by the term 'case study'. Here, there is no universally accepted definition, but the one given by Fred Percival and Henry Ellington in 1980 is probably as good as any: 'an in-depth examination of a real-life or simulated situation carried out to illustrate special and/or general characteristics'. Thus, to qualify as a 'case study', an exercise must again have two essential features, namely, *in-depth study* carried out in order to *illustrate particular characteristics*.

The above definition probably includes most things that readers would regard as constituting 'case studies'. Also note that the 'particular characteristics' being illustrated can either be special characteristics specific to the case being examined or more general features of the broader set of which it is a member; case studies are used to illustrate both types of characteristics.

Classification of exercises by 'function'

Since the early 1970s, it has been increasingly recognized that games, simulations and case studies are in fact closely inter-related. Indeed, it is now accepted that they form broad overlapping sets that can be represented by a Venn diagram of the type shown in Figure 1.1.

We can see from Figure 1.1 that there are at least seven distinct types of exercise within the game/simulation/case-study field, namely, three 'pure' types and four 'hybrid' types. Let us now illustrate these by means of examples.

1. *'Pure' games.* These are exercises which possess both of the essential characteristics of games (*competition* and *rules*) but not those of simulations or case studies. *Scrabble* and *football* are two well-known examples, as are familiar card games such as *bridge, rummy* and *poker*.
2. *'Pure' simulations.* These are exercises which have the essential characteristics of simulations (ie, are ongoing representations of real situations) but not of games or case studies. Training simulators such as the *Link Trainer* developed during the Second World War to teach basic flying skills are good examples of the genre, as are many computer simulations and 'virtual reality' situations.

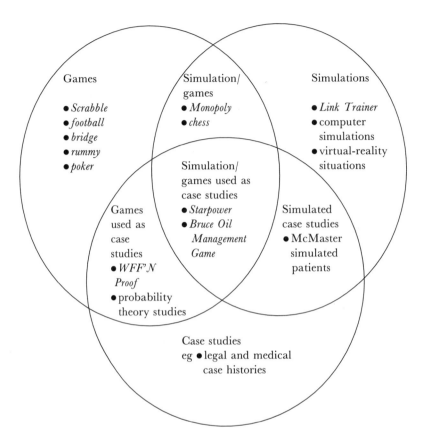

Figure 1.1 The overlapping sets of games, simulations and case studies.

3. *'Pure' case studies.* These are exercises which have the essential features of case studies (in-depth study carried out to illustrate special character-istics) but not of games or simulations. Conventional legal and medical case studies fall into this category.

4. *Simulation/games.* These are exercises which have all the essential features of both games *and* simulations, but not of case studies. *Monopoly* is a well-known example of the genre, as is *chess*, which is based on a battle in eighth-century India (how many people realize that the moves of the rook simulate those of the war elephant?).

5. *Games used as case studies.* These are exercises which have all the essential characteristics of games *and* case studies, but not of simulations. A good example is *WFF'N Proof* – a game that was developed at the University of Michigan for use in the teaching of symbolic logic and mathematics. Further examples include the use of simple gambling games (such as coin-tossing and craps) as case studies in probability theory.

6. *Simulated case studies.* These are exercises which have the essential features of both simulations *and* case studies but not of games. The 'simulated patient' technique developed at McMaster University in Canada for use in medical training is a well-known example, as are virtual-reality operations (as in veterinary procedures) and virtual-reality tours (as in architectural design) in which parameters can be varied.

7. *Simulation/games used as case studies.* These are exercises which have all the essential features of games, simulations *and* case studies. Examples are *Starpower* (a well-known simulation of social class conflict that was developed at the Western Behavioral Sciences Institute in California during the late 1960s) and *The Bruce Oil Management Game* (a computer-based business game that was developed in Robert Gordon's Institute of Technology during the 1970s). Both will be described later in this book.

Classification of exercises by 'format'

In addition to the above classification by *function* (ie, in terms of the way in which they are used) games, simulations and case studies are often classified by *format* (ie, in terms of the medium in which they are presented). Here, the most important distinction is between *manual exercises* (which do not involve the use of a computer or other electronic data-processing system) and *electronic exercises* (which do involve the use of such devices). In developing this sort of classification, it is possible to use similar hierarchical taxonomies to those used to classify living things. Figure 1.2 gives some indication of how this might be done.

We can see from Figure 1.2 that manual exercises can be subdivided into basic classes such as simple manual exercises (those which involve the use of no specialized materials other than briefing sheets, role cards, etc), card games (that involve the use of a specialized pack or packs of cards), board games (that are played on a special board of some sort), and so on. These basic classes, in turn, can be further subdivided and sub-subdivided until we eventually come down to individual exercises such as *chess* and *Scrabble*. Electronic exercises can be classified in a similar way. We have, however, resisted the temptation to develop an all-embracing format-based classification of the game/simulation/case-study field, since this is meant to be a practical book for teachers rather than a theoretical book for academics. We leave it to some latter-day Linnaeus or budding Bloom to produce the definitive version of such a taxonomy. No doubt there is a PhD (or at least a 'Masters' degree) in it for whoever manages to see the task through!

Exercises of the game/simulation/case study type

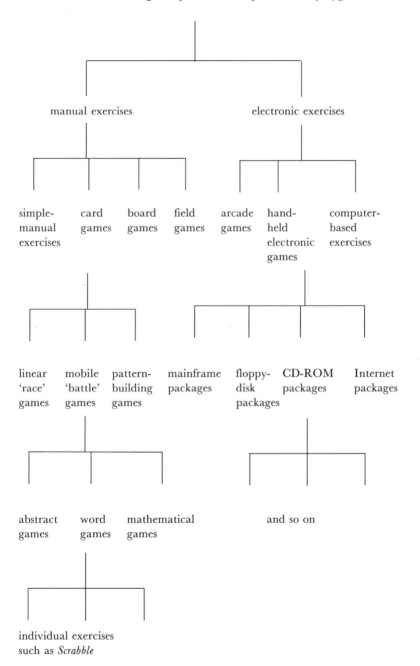

Figure 1.2 The hierarchical classification of games, simulations and case studies.

2

Some General Educational Features of Games and Simulations

Let us now take a general look at some of the basic educational characteristics of games and simulations, analysing their strengths and weaknesses and identifying some of the main educational contexts in which they can be used.

Some of the educational strengths of games and simulations

There are a number of reasons why games and simulations are useful from an educational point of view, some of the most important of which are listed below.

- First, games and simulations constitute a highly versatile and flexible medium whereby a wide range of *cognitive objectives* covering all six levels of Bloom's cognitive domain can be achieved. Although research has shown that such techniques are no more effective than traditional methods in teaching the basic facts and principles of a subject, they have been found to be particularly useful in reinforcing the teaching of such facts and principles, and in providing useful case studies and enhancement experiences. They are also particularly effective in achieving higher-cognitive objectives of all types, ie in developing pupils' powers of application, analysis, synthesis and evaluation.

- Games and simulations are also ideal vehicles for developing the *transferable process skills* that have become such an important part of all levels of education since the early 1980s, especially in Britain, where their development has become a key part of government policy. They are particularly well suited for developing decision-making, problem-solving, interpersonal and communication skills – the sort of skills that employers are increasingly coming to expect in the products of our education systems.

- One of the main reasons why games and simulations have achieved such widespread use since the late 1960s is that they fitted in well with the move towards *pupil-centred learning* that was triggered by the humanistic psychology school at roughly the same time. Classroom games and simulations are ideal vehicles for facilitating such learning, since they are, by their very nature, strongly 'pupil-centred'.

- In many cases, exercises of the game/simulation/case-study type also constitute vehicles whereby pupils can use their *initiative* and develop their powers of *creative thought*. This characteristic is again proving particularly important as our educational systems continue to place progressively greater emphasis on the cultivation of divergent thought processes.

- Games, simulations and case studies are also extremely effective vehicles for achieving *affective objectives* of all types, eg encouraging pupils to listen to other people's points of view, or to appreciate that most real-life problems can generally be viewed in a number of different ways.

- In exercises where some sort of *competition* is involved (not necessarily at the expense of cooperation), this can provide powerful motivation for the participants to commit themselves wholeheartedly to the work involved. This competitive element may be overt (when individuals or groups are in open competition with one another), or it may be covert (as, for example, when individuals or groups have to perform parallel activities and report their findings to the class as a whole).

- Basing the scenario of an exercise on a simulated situation as opposed to a real-life situation allows the scenario and the associated learning experiences to be tailored to the desired educational objectives rather than being constrained by the actual features of the situation. Only very rarely does a real-life situation have all the features that the designer of a case study wishes to bring out, whereas a simulated situation can have all such features built in. Also, real-life situations are often much too complicated to be used as the basis of an educational exercise as they stand; the simplification that the use of simulations allows can often overcome this difficulty by reducing the complexity to manageable proportions.

- Many games and simulations have a basis in more than one academic discipline, a feature that can help the participants to integrate concepts from otherwise widely related areas into a cohesive and balanced 'world picture'. Exercises which require pupils to formulate value judgements (for example, weighing economic benefits against social or environmental costs) or examine problems from a number of different perspectives are particularly valuable in this respect.

- Multi-disciplinary exercises have an additional advantage in that they can provide a situation in which participants with expertise in different subject areas have to work together effectively in order to achieve a common end. Interpersonal skills of this type are very important in later life, and constitute an area of education and training in which the multi-disciplinary simulation and simulation/game may well be the only means of providing practical experience in a school or college environment.

- Finally, one universally observed advantage of game/simulation/case-study techniques is that pupil involvement and motivation are very high – features that are particularly beneficial when using these techniques with the less able. In addition, most participants find the approach extremely enjoyable.

Some of the educational weaknesses of such exercises

Exercises of the game/simulation/case-study type do also have some possible educational disadvantages and it is important that all potential users should be aware of these.

- First, running such exercises can pose a number of *organizational problems*, particularly at secondary school and college levels, where teachers generally have to work to a strict, externally-imposed timetable rather than having virtually complete control over their pupils' day-to-day activities, as is the case at nursery and primary level. This can make it difficult to fit games and simulations into the curriculum, particularly if they take a long time to run or require special facilities or accommodation.

- A second potential weakness of educational games and simulations is that they require the *active cooperation* of the participants if they are to succeed. In some cases, however, this cooperation may not be forthcoming. Although most pupils enjoy taking part in games and simulations, some do not. Pupils may, for example simply not turn up for the session because they feel that it may be a waste of time or are afraid of taking part. In other cases, they may be reluctant to make the very real personal commitment that many games and simulations require, because they do not feel that they have the necessary skills, or do not want to 'show themselves up' in front of their peers. These problems tend to be much more serious in secondary schools and colleges than in nursery and primary schools, but have to be addressed and overcome if an exercise is to be run successfully.

- Third, there is always a danger of using such exercises for the wrong reasons – using them as 'diversions' or 'time fillers' rather than for some specific educational purpose. Also, with some so-called 'educational games', it is possible for pupils to play them purely as games, without deriving any worthwhile educational benefit, because the 'educational' and 'gaming' elements are not fully integrated. A number of commercially available card and board games tend to have this weakness, as do many computer games and simulations. Thus, it is vitally important that any teacher considering using a game or simulation with a class should make sure that it will help to achieve worthwhile educational objectives. Designing your own exercises rather than using other people's can help ensure that this is indeed the case. (Guidance on how to do this will be given later in the book.)

- An associated problem is that of ensuring that the *level* of an educational game or simulation is properly matched to the ability and needs of the group of pupils with which it is to be used. Unfortunately, it is very unusual to find a ready-made exercise that is *ideally* suited to the purpose that the teacher has in mind. Thus, it is often necessary to carry out a certain amount of adaptation or modification before using an exercise with a class. (Guidance on how to do this will again be given later.)
- Finally, there are a number of very real problems specifically associated with the use of computer-based games and simulations in schools. Many teachers feel uncomfortable using such exercises at all because they themselves lack the necessary IT skills, or are afraid of revealing their limited skills to their increasingly IT-literate pupils. There is also the perennial problem of keeping up to date with the latest technology and courseware developments, which often mean that a package or piece of kit purchased one year can be out of date the next. Indeed, as budgets become progressively tighter, there is a very real danger that some less-well-off schools will simply give up on the serious use of computer-based learning, and revert to more traditional teaching and learning methods.

Educational contexts in which games and simulations can be used

Let us now examine some of the specific educational contexts within which teachers can use games and simulations in their classrooms.

To develop language and communication skills

Possibly the area in which games and simulations can make their greatest contribution to education at school level is in helping children to develop their *language and communication skills*. As we will see in Chapter 4, well-designed classroom games can help children attending nursery school to develop the listening and spoken-language skills that are such an essential preparation for the development of reading and writing skills once they move on to the early stages of their primary education. When they do, games and simulations can play a key role in helping them to develop the basic reading and writing skills that constitute the foundations of literacy, as we will see in Chapter 5. As will be shown in Chapters 6 and 7, games and simulations can continue to make a valuable contribution to the enhancement and refinement of the developing child's spoken and written communication skills all the way through the remainder of their formal education and, indeed, beyond this. Numerous examples of exercises that include the development of spoken and written communication skills in their educational objectives are described in these chapters.

To develop pre-maths, number and computational skills

Educational games and simulations can make a similarly valuable contribution to the development of the growing child's numerical and computational skills. As we will see in Chapter 4, the process can again begin at nursery level, where games and simulations can be used to help children develop the various shape-recognition, pattern-recognition and other skills that lay the foundations for the acquisition of basic numeracy. In Chapter 5, we will show how games and simulations can play a key role in helping them to develop such numeracy within a challenging and highly motivating context. Chapters 6 and 7 will then demonstrate how games and simulations can be used to help older children to apply, enhance and further develop their computational skills – again in highly motivating and enjoyable situations that relate to the real world in which they will eventually have to make a living.

To develop IT skills

To survive in tomorrow's 'information age', today's children are going to have to become fully *computer literate* and develop *IT skills* to a level that can barely be imagined by most of their parents. Once again, games and simulations can play a key role in helping them to do so. Children now start playing computer games in nursery schools, and, by the time they move on to primary school, are already often much more at home with computers than the people who are teaching them. Figure 2.1 shows children from Towie Primary School in Aberdeenshire using a computer simulation to predict Britain's likely future use of energy. Primary children now carry out such work as a matter of routine, as do children studying many subjects at secondary level. As we will see in Chapters 5–7, acquaintance with computer games and simulations can

Figure 2.1 Primary pupils using a computer simulation to predict likely future energy consumption in Britain.

play a crucial part in helping them to develop their IT skills as they move through the educational system and, again, does so in a highly motivating and enjoyable context. With the ever-increasing opportunities now becoming available via the Internet, who knows what can be achieved by the use of such techniques.

To reinforce the teaching of basic facts and principles

As we have seen, exercises of the game/simulation/case-study type offer no advantages over more traditional methods such as face-to-face teaching and directed self-study in teaching the basic facts and principles of a subject. They can, however, be extremely effective in reinforcing the teaching of such basic facts and principles, in demonstrating applications and in providing illustrative case studies. Practically all the games and simulations described in Chapters 4–7 help to achieve objectives of this general type, a good example being the *Formulon* card game examined in Chapter 7 (see Figure 2.2). This is designed to reinforce basic teaching on the chemical properties of different types of elements and ions and the way in which these combine to form chemical compounds. The game enables pupils to apply their knowledge in a highly motivating, competitive situation, and, through feedback from other players and from the supervising teacher, helps players to fill any gaps in their knowledge or correct any fundamental misunderstandings that they may have.

Figure 2.2 Secondary pupils using *Formulon* to reinforce their knowledge of how elements and ions combine to form chemical compounds.

To develop higher-cognitive skills of all types

We have seen that games, simulations and case studies are extremely effective in helping pupils to develop *higher-cognitive skills* of all types. They are particularly effective in developing multi-faceted skills related to such things as problem-solving, decision-making and creative thinking, and, in such areas, probably constitute one of the most powerful weapons in our educational armoury. Many of the games described in Chapters 5–7 are designed to achieve objectives of this type, the *Power for Pemang* simulation/game described in Chapter 7 being an excellent example of the genre. This requires pupils to come up with a strategy for meeting the future electricity needs of an imaginary island, and involves the use of all the different types of higher-cognitive skill listed above. Other good examples of exercises that are specifically designed to develop such skills are the *Amsyn Problem* and *Oil Strike Huntly* simulation/games also described in Chapter 7.

To support and supplement conventional laboratory work

Simulations and simulated case studies can be used as a *supplement to*, and, in some cases, as a *substitute for, conventional laboratory work*. The various types of mechanical or electronic training simulator have, of course, a long history of use in laboratories of all types, but the universal availability of microcomputers now means that students can be given direct experience (through simulations) of a far wider range of experimental situations than was feasible before. Specific areas where such computer-based simulations can be used include:

- situations where a conventional experiment is either extremely difficult or impossible (eg experiments in astrophysics and human genetics, and 'thought experiments' such as the investigation of non-inverse-square gravitation)
- Situations where experimental apparatus is either not readily available or too complicated or expensive for general laboratory use (eg experiments in reactor physics and industrial processes of all kinds)
- Situations where actual experimental work could be dangerous (eg work with explosive mixtures, highly radioactive materials, toxic chemicals, virulent pathogens, etc)
- Situations where a conventional experiment would take an unacceptably long time to complete (eg experiments in genetics, sociology or population dynamics).

Computer simulations can also be used to allow pupils to 'try out' experiments before they carry them out 'for real', eg designing electronic circuits, machines or buildings. Such computer-aided design now plays a key role in the teaching of a wide range of subjects, especially at upper-secondary and post-school level.

To develop interpersonal and social skills

Another area in which participative exercises of the game/simulation/case-study type have proved extremely effective is in helping pupils to develop the various *interpersonal and social skills* that they need in order to succeed in the outside world. As we will see in Chapters 4–7, they can be used in this role at all levels of education from nursery school upwards. Role-playing simulations are found to be particularly effective in developing interpersonal and social skills, since they can be used to give pupils experience of what it actually feels like to find themselves in a wide range of situations. Exercises such as the *Barter* game described in Chapter 6 (which gives pupils a feel for what it is like to live in a society where barter is the main means of exchange) and the *Starpower* simulation/game described in Chapter 7 (which shows them how stratification and conflict almost inevitably develop in an uncontrolled free-enterprise society) are typical examples of the genre.

To develop psychomotor skills

Games and simulations can also be used to help pupils develop *psychomotor skills* of various types. At nursery and lower-primary level they can be used to help children to develop basic manipulative and placing skills and the motor skills associated with learning to write (see Chapters 4 and 5). Higher up the school, involving pupils in the design of games and simulations can provide an extremely effective context to help them develop a wide range of graphic and artistic skills (see Chapter 10). Games and simulations can also be used to help pupils develop more specific psychomotor skills such as keyboard skills and the skills associated with cooking. The detailed case study given at the end of Chapter 5 provides a good example of their use for the latter purpose.

To develop multi-faceted skills related to real life

Simulations, simulation/games and simulated case studies are also extremely useful vehicles to help students develop a wide range of multi-faceted work-related skills and competences. The development of such skills and competences is now being regarded as an increasingly important part of the preparation of pupils to participate in the world of work. A good example of the type of exercise that can be used for such a purpose is the production of a class newspaper, as described in Chapter 6. Here, the members of the class act as a multi-disciplinary team, taking on all the various roles that are associated with the production of a 'real' newspaper (editor, reporters, production staff, and so on). In so doing, they learn a great deal about what the actual job entails, and also gain first-hand experience of the importance of things like team-working and working to deadlines. They also pick up a wide range of work-related skills, including IT skills of various types.

To achieve affective objectives of all types

The general area of *affective development* – helping pupils to develop desirable and flexible attitudinal traits such as open-mindedness, empathy and willingness to appreciate other people's points of view – is all too often neglected in formal education because most affective objectives are rather difficult to achieve. It has, however, been found that games, simulations and case studies can be extremely effective in achieving such objectives, since they give the pupils the opportunity to experience the situation being examined, and to feel what it is like to find one's self in a particular role. Exercises that incorporate role reversal, and force people to confront a particular situation from a different perspective from that which they would normally adopt, are particularly powerful in this regard. Chapters 5–7 describe a number of exercises that include affective development among their aims and objectives. These include the *Road Safety Ludo* game described in Chapter 5, one of whose main aims is to help pupils develop a proper attitude to road safety. Another is the *Starpower* simulation/game described in Chapter 6, which is designed to help pupils develop social awareness and an appreciation of how social inequality can lead to conflict. Yet another is the *Amsyn Problem* exercise described in Chapter 7, which is designed to show pupils how real-life problems can be viewed from a number of totally different perspectives, and how their successful resolution requires the points of view of all the interested parties to be taken into account.

How games and simulations can be used for staff development purposes

Games and simulations can also play a useful role in the development of staff within schools and colleges. They can, for example, be used to help to promote teambuilding, to help staff develop a wide range of useful skills, and to make them aware of the power and effectiveness of games and simulations as teaching tools. When the 1990–91 Grampian Primary Industry Project was being launched, all the teachers who had expressed an interest in participating were invited to a staff-development day held in a local hotel. Here, they were given a talk on the educational uses of games and simulations, and then spent the rest of the morning taking part in an actual simulation/game – the *North Sea Auction* exercise that is described in detail at the end of Chapter 3 (see Figure 2.3). This gave them first-hand experience of what participating in such an exercise involves, and fully convinced everyone who took part of the great educational value of games and simulations.

Once the staff of a given school have been introduced to the use of games and simulations, they can be actively involved in the selection of suitable exercises for use with their pupils (eg, by trying out possible games) and can also design custom-built exercises for use with their classes. The work carried out in Scotland's Grampian Region in connection with the Grampian Primary Industry Project and the ensuing programme of staff development and dissemination that it gave rise to clearly showed that virtually all class teachers have the skills needed to design effective classroom games, provided they are given a little basic training and have their confidence boosted. The guidance given in Chapters 8–10 of this book should be more than sufficient for this purpose. These describe two possible approaches to the design of classroom games and simulations, and also demonstrate the additional educational advantages that can accrue from involving the pupils themselves in the design of such exercises.

As will be shown in the detailed case studies on the use of games and simulations in teaching major parts of the curriculum in Chapters 4–7, the process of developing such exercises can itself make a major contribution to the development of the staff involved. All the projects described involved identifying an area of the curriculum to which games or simulations could

Figure 2.3 One of the teams of teachers at the launch of the Grampian Primary Industry Project preparing their 'company bid' for the *North Sea Auction* game, watched by the game facilitator, Henry Ellington.

make a significant contribution, carrying out all the background research and other preparatory work needed to develop suitable exercises, and then developing the exercises themselves. In all four of the case studies described, this 'R & D' work involved establishing links with appropriate sectors of industry or commerce, links which themselves played a key role in the success of the projects. Indeed, combining the development of classroom games and simulations with the development of links with the outside world is a doubly effective strategy that is strongly commended to all teachers.

3

Choosing and Using Games and Simulations

Some Basic Guidelines

Having explained what games and simulations are and examined their basic educational characteristics, let us now turn to more practical aspects of their classroom use – how to choose suitable exercises for specific educational purposes and how to use them effectively with a class of pupils.

Choosing a game or simulation for a specific purpose

The authors have found that this is best done by working through the following three stages.

1. Establish your objectives.
2. Decide what type of exercise to use.
3. Choose a specific exercise.

Stage 1 Establishing your objectives

Before you start to think about choosing an exercise, you should be quite clear as to the job that you want the exercise to do. This is best done by asking yourself the following questions:

- With whom is the exercise to be used?
- For what basic purpose?
- What specific educational objectives or learning outcomes do you want to achieve?

Games, simulations and case studies can be used for a wide range of purposes, so it is important that you establish the specific educational purposes that you have in mind.

Stage 2 Deciding what type of exercise to use

Once you have established your educational objectives or learning outcomes, you should then give some thought as to what type of exercise you think would be best suited to helping you to achieve these. Specifically, you should ask yourself the following questions:

- What basic type of exercise do you think would be suitable? (A case study? A simulation/game? A role-playing simulation?)
- What format of exercise do you want to use? (A simple manual exercise? A board game? A computer simulation?)

Stage 3 Choosing a specific exercise

Once you have made up your mind about the basic type and format of the exercise that you would like to use, you should then set about the task of seeing whether exercises of the type you want are in fact available, and, if so, choosing the one that you feel would be most suitable to meet your needs. The tasks should again be tackled by seeking the answers to a number of questions.

- Is an exercise (manual or electronic) of the type you want available 'in house', ie within your own establishment or within any larger organization of which it forms a part? (If it is, get hold of it and use it.)
- If a suitable exercise is not available 'in house', could such an exercise be obtained from an external source? Here, probably the best advice that can be given to would-be users of games, simulations and case studies is to get in touch with *SAGSET*, the *Society for Interactive Learning* – formerly, the Society for the Advancement of Games and Simulations in Education and Training (Gala House, 3 Raglan Road, Edgbaston, Birmingham B5 7RA, UK). SAGSET produce a series of resource lists, each of which gives details of the materials that are currently available in a particular discipline or subject area. These lists represent an invaluable bank of information, and are highly recommended to anyone who wishes to make use of games or simulations. An alternative approach is to carry out an on-line search of the World Wide Web, on which an ever-increasing number of databases covering virtually all topics – including games and simulations – are being established. The various catalogues that are produced by the manufacturers and publishers of games, simulations and computer packages are also a rich source of up-to-date information on what is currently available. Indeed, in the case of computer-based and multimedia packages, where new products are becoming available practically every week, they are probably the best place to look for ideas.

If you find that an exercise of the type you want is *not* available 'in house' or from an external source, you have three options available to you:

1. Forget about using a game or simulation, and think of some other way of achieving your objectives.
2. Try to find an existing exercise that you can adapt to meet your needs. (Detailed practical guidance on how to do this is given in the next section.)
3. Design your own custom-built exercise 'from scratch'. (Detailed practical guidance on how to do this is given in Chapters 8 –10.)

Carrying out any modifications needed

When looking for an exercise to fulfil a specific function, it is very unusual to find one that meets your needs exactly. You are much more likely to find an exercise that is roughly what you want, but cannot be used in its existing form for one or more of the following reasons:

●   The level is wrong (ie the degree of difficulty or complexity is either too high or too low for the pupils with which you plan to use it).
●   The length is wrong (ie the exercise is either too long or too short for the intended mode of use).
●   The logistics are unsuitable as they stand (eg the exercise is designed for a different number of participants from that envisaged, or is intended for a different mode of use).
●   The balance of the objectives is not really suitable for achieving the particular outcomes you have in mind (eg there may be too much emphasis on content and not enough on process, or vice versa).
●   The content is not really appropriate for the pupils you wish to work with, although the general format and structure are just about right.
●   The scenario on which the exercise is based has become outdated, thus reducing the realism (and hence the credibility) of the exercise.

Some basic approaches to the modification process

The authors have found that there are four basic ways in which an exercise can be modified in order to meet specific user needs, ranging from making comparatively minor changes to carrying out a radical re-write. Clearly, it is advisable to explore the easier options first, only embarking on the last if this is really necessary. The four strategies are:

1. Use the existing package in a different way from that envisaged by the designer. Remember that when you acquire an educational or training

package such as a simulation/game, you are under no legal or moral obligation to use it in the way the author suggests. It is, after all, simply an educational resource that you may elect to use in any way that you see fit.

2.   Modify the package by changing the number of items used, eg by not using some items at all if you feel that they do not fit in with your plans, by not using all the copies of a particular item if you are running the exercise with a smaller number of people than that envisaged by the designer, or by producing additional copies of particular items if the package does not contain enough for the number of participants with whom you wish to use the exercise.

3.   Modify the package to meet your needs by changing some or all of the resource materials without radically altering the content or structure of the exercise as a whole, eg by making slight changes to the scenario in order to make it more suitable for the pupils with whom you wish to use the exercise.

4.   Carry out a radical re-write or re-design of the exercise, eg by retaining the existing content but changing the structure, by retaining the existing structure but changing the content, or by changing both the content and the structure.

Needless to say, you should make sure that you are not infringing the law of copyright when carrying out any of the above modifications. If you wrote the original package yourself, there will generally be no problems here. If you are modifying someone else's package, on the other hand, you will obviously have to be a little more careful, but will probably be in the clear if you only intend to use the revised package yourself. Only if you intend to make the revised package generally available, or publish it commercially, are any serious problems likely to arise. In such cases, you would almost certainly have to obtain the permission of the copyright holder before proceeding. If in doubt, seek legal advice on the matter.

How to carry out different types of modification

Let us now take a detailed look at how to modify a game or simulation in order to solve the different types of compatibility problem identified earlier.

Reducing the level of difficulty of an exercise

This is a common problem faced by designers and users of games and simulations, particularly if they wish to run an exercise with younger pupils than those for whom it was originally written. A number of things can be done in order to make an exercise less difficult, eg:

- simplify the exercise by making it shorter, eg by removing any stages not regarded as essential
- remove any processes or materials that you consider to be beyond the capabilities of the participants you have in mind
- provide the participants with additional help or guidelines, particularly with the more difficult parts
- break the exercise down into discrete, manageable stages
- require a lower level of performance in the exercise as a whole or in some of the individual stages.

Increasing the level of difficulty of an exercise

Contrary to what some readers might expect, this is (in the authors' experience at any rate) usually somewhat easier than reducing the level of difficulty. Measures that can be taken in order to bring such a change about include the following:

- add new, more demanding material, processes or stages
- provide less help to the participants, eg by making them search for key information in the resource documents rather than pointing it out to them, making them calculate data for themselves rather than simply providing it, and leaving them to work out how to carry out calculations rather than giving them detailed instructions
- require a higher level of performance, eg by increasing the time available for certain stages, specifying the standards that have to be reached, and providing more critical debriefing.

Reducing the length of an exercise

Another problem that is frequently encountered by would-be users of educational games and simulations is that of fitting an exercise into a time slot that is too short to run the exercise as it stands. Assuming that a shorter exercise of the same general type is not readily available, the obvious solution is to reduce the length of the exercise in question. The task is similar to that of reducing the level of difficulty of an exercise, and can be tackled in a number of ways:

- reduce the number of stages that the exercise involves, provided that this can be done without losing its overall integrity and educational value
- make the exercise easier, with the same caveat as above
- require a lower level of performance in the exercise as a whole or in selected stages, again with the same caveat.

Increasing the length of an exercise

If an exercise is too short for the time slot in which it is intended to run, it is usually a comparatively simple matter to increase its length. Two of the ways in which this can be done are as follows:

- increase the number of stages by sub-dividing existing stages or adding completely new activities
- allow more time for some or all of the existing stages, and require a correspondingly higher level of performance.

Changing the logistics of an exercise

Changing the logistics of an exercise to accommodate a different number of participants from that for which it was originally intended, or to enable it to be used in a different way from that envisaged by the designer, can be an extremely simple task or an extremely complicated one, depending on the circumstances. Some of the measures that can be employed in order to do so are:

- change the numbers of individual resource items to suit the new mode of use
- add supplementary or completely new resource items if necessary
- change the organizational structure in order to fit in with the new context of use.

Changing the balance of the objectives of an exercise

If a game or simulation is to be used with a different group of people from that for which it was originally designed, it is often found that the balance of the objectives is not quite right. The exercise may, for example, be strongly content-based when what is required is a greater emphasis on process, or, conversely, may be a highly process-centred exercise that does not have enough 'hard' content for the particular target group you have in mind. Again, a number of standard techniques can be used to adjust the balance in the way required, eg:

- modify the structure of the exercise by removing unwanted stages or adding new stages
- change the level of performance required in specific stages of the exercise to reflect what is required
- simply alter the timing of the exercise.

Changing the content of an exercise

When trying to choose a game or simulation for a particular purpose, you sometimes manage to find one that is just what you are looking for with regard to format and structure, but is not quite so suitable from the content point of view. In such cases, it is often possible to remedy matters by doing one of the following:

- modify the existing content so that it is more appropriate to your needs
- change to a completely new content.

Updating the scenario of an exercise

A problem with which both designers and users of educational games and simulations are regularly confronted is that of keeping their exercises up to date, so that they are perceived as relevant by the people who are playing them. This is particularly important in the case of exercises that involve costs or other economic factors, since these can become outdated very quickly, particularly in times of high inflation. Scenarios can also become outdated by new technical developments, or by unforeseen events such as the Chernobyl and Challenger disasters. Measures that can be taken to overcome such problems include the following:

- keep the existing scenario up to date without introducing any radical changes, eg by simply updating costs, prices, etc as and when required
- carry out qualitative changes to the scenario to reflect any important technological or other developments
- remove the 'perishable' content of the scenario completely.

Preparing to run an exercise

Let us assume that you have found a game or simulation suitable for the purpose you have in mind, or have produced such an exercise by modifying one that already exists or designing your own. You should now carry out any preparatory work that is required before you actually run the exercise with your pupils. This can be broken down into the following tasks.

- Make sure that the package of resource materials is available and complete. If any materials are missing, try to get hold of replacements; if necessary, make up your own. Take special care to ensure that there are enough copies of any pupil resource materials (briefing sheets, role sheets, etc) to cater for all the people who will be taking part. If necessary, run off additional copies.
- Make sure that all other facilities needed for running the exercise will be available as and when required (eg accommodation, audiovisual or computer facilities, extra staff or facilitators). This is particularly important in the case of a computer-based exercise, where it is absolutely essential to ensure (a) that a sufficient number of workstations are

available to run the exercise with the number of pupils who will be taking part, and (b) that the game or simulation package runs properly on all of these. If the exercise is being run on multiple workstations via a file server, make sure that your distribution system is working properly. Also, check that you have the necessary licence to run the exercise with multiple users (many teachers tend to forget about this legal side of things!).

- Check that you will have a suitable number of participants to ensure that the exercise can be run effectively (if necessary, 'borrow' pupils from another class in order to make up the numbers). This is particularly important in the case of role-playing simulation/games, structured debates and similar manual exercises where it is absolutely essential that all the key participants are present. In such cases, you are strongly advised to have contingency plans to cope with any unexpected absences, eg by having suitable 'understudies' available or by being ready to take on any such role(s) yourself.

- Make yourself thoroughly familiar with the complete package, and, in particular, with the 'organizer's guide', if one is supplied. If such a guide is not included in the package, it is strongly recommended that you prepare your own, as this will be extremely helpful in sorting out your ideas and plans. Such an organizer's guide should cover the following areas:

    - It should specify the *educational objectives* of the exercise, so that would-be users have a clear idea of the purposes for which it can be used.
    - It should specify the *type of pupils* with whom the exercise is suitable for use, and, if necessary, specify any particular knowledge or skills they will need in order to participate effectively.
    - It should provide any *background information* that the teacher will need in order to prepare for or run the exercise, eg any material needed to carry out any preliminary teaching necessary, to brief the participants at the start of the exercise itself, or to debrief the participants once the exercise is over.
    - It should list the *materials and facilities* needed to run the exercise, so that anyone who has to do so can use it as a 'check list' to ensure that everything is available.
    - It should provide *detailed instructions or guidelines* on how to prepare to run the exercise, how to actually run the exercise, and how to carry out any debriefing or follow-up work necessary.

The detailed guidelines on how to run *North Sea Auction* with a class that are given at the end of this chapter provide a good example of such an organizer's guide.

- Carry out any preliminary teaching that may be necessary. In some cases, the exercise will simply be a natural follow-up to work that you would be carrying out as part of the normal class curriculum, so no special teaching will be required. In other cases, it will be necessary to give the class a special lesson – or even a series of lessons – on the subject matter on which the game or simulation is based, so that the pupils are fully prepared to take an effective part. Before running *North Sea Auction*, for example, it would probably be advisable to carry out some preliminary teaching on the nature and origins of oil, where it is found, how oil companies explore for oil, and so on.

- Issue any introductory or background material, and make sure that the participants know what the exercise will involve; if necessary, allocate pupils to roles (or groups) and issue any briefing or resource material. It is particularly important to make sure that any weaker or less able pupils are properly briefed on what they will have to do, and are given any encouragement and support needed to ensure that they do not feel threatened or insecure, and that they perform to the best of their ability.

All these points may seem rather obvious (especially to those with some experience of running games and simulations) but they are all essential if the exercise is to run smoothly.

Running a game or simulation with a class

Just how you set about running a game or simulation with a class will depend on the nature of the exercise and the specific educational context in which it is being used. It is, however, important to realize that your role as a teacher and the roles of your pupils will almost certainly be radically different from your respective roles in a conventional 'taught lesson'. In such a lesson, you are (or should be!) firmly in control at all times, determining what is being taught, how it is taught, at what pace, and with what degree of interaction with the pupils. This mode of teaching has been described as the *dependent mode*, since the pupils are almost totally dependent on what they get from the teacher. All teachers tend to be perfectly happy and comfortable working in this mode, since they are all completely familiar with it.

If the game or simulation that you will be using with your class is designed for use by individual pupils (eg is an individual puzzle such as a crossword or an individual computer exercise of some sort), then you will be required to operate in a completely different mode. Here, your role will be the same as when running any other individualized-learning activity with a class, namely, a producer/manager of learning resources, and a tutor/guide, providing help, support and encouragement to individual pupils as and when required (see Figure 3.1). In such a mode, the pupils are largely responsible for their own

Figure 3.1 A primary teacher supervising children carrying out individual work, ie working in the 'independent mode'.

learning, with individual pupils controlling their own pace of learning, depth of study, etc. For these reasons, the individualized-learning mode has been described as the *independent mode*. All teachers (especially nursery and primary teachers) again tend to be completely happy and comfortable when working in this mode, since they are again completely familiar with it.

If the game or simulation is designed to be played by groups of pupils, on the other hand, as is the case with the great majority of exercises of this type, your role will again be completely different. It will, in fact, be that of organizer of the group activity and facilitator of the student learning experience. In such exercises, the pupils will again be largely responsible for their own learning, but will also be strongly dependent on one another for the overall quality of their individual learning experiences. For these reasons, the group-learning mode has been described as the *interdependent mode*. Some teachers, particularly older teachers who are accustomed to operating in more traditional modes, feel uncomfortable in this mode, since it requires them to stand back and let their pupils get on with it, only intervening when this is deemed to be absolutely necessary. Indeed, when carrying out a group activity such as playing a game or tackling a group problem, the pupils often do not want to have any interaction with the teacher at all. Figure 3.2 shows secondary pupils engaged in such group work, as part of an extended role-playing simulation game. This particular group actually told the game organizer to keep out of their way unless they specifically asked for help!

Figure 3.2 Secondary pupils working in the 'interdependent mode' as part of an extended role-playing simulation/game.

One other important point should be borne in mind by anyone running a game or simulation with a class. Unless you are deliberately departing from the method of organization recommended by the designer, make sure that you follow the instructions given in the organizer's guide. This is particularly important in the case of a complex or multi-stage exercise, where keeping to the 'game plan' is essential if things are to run smoothly. With such exercises, it is especially important to make sure that the various stages run to time.

Following up on the experience

Practically all workers in the gaming and simulation field agree that a *debriefing* session of some sort is essential if full educational value is to be derived from a game, simulation or case study. The form of this debriefing will depend on the nature of the exercise involved and the context in which it is being used, but should generally include the following three elements.

- Review of the *actual work of the exercise*, and discussion of any important points that are brought up by the participants.
- Discussion of the *relationship* between the exercise and the subject matter on which it is based (eg discussion of the degree of realism of the exercise in the case of a simulation).
- Discussion of any *broader issues* raised by the exercise.

If the exercise was itself being tested in any way (eg if you were trying out a newly modified version of an existing game or simulation), a fourth element should be included, namely, discussion of possible methods by which it could be *improved*.

The debriefing session is particularly important in the case of exercises that involve role-play or place the intrinsic subject matter in a social, political, economic or environmental context; indeed, in these cases, it is often the most important part of the entire exercise. A good example of such an exercise is the *Starpower* simulation/game described in Chapter 7. As we will see, this is a simulation of the development of a three-tiered 'capitalist' society in which the social class to which you belong depends on how successful you are in the economic 'game' on which such a society is based. The overall objective of the game is to arrive at a situation in which the 'have-nots' rebel against the domination and autocracy of the 'haves', causing the trading activity on which it is based to break down because of its intrinsic unfairness (the trading rules are increasingly controlled by the 'haves'). Once such a breakdown has occurred, it is the role of the game facilitator to 'calm things down' and draw out the key lessons that the participants are expected to learn from their experience.

With some exercises, it may also be necessary for the teacher to carry out follow-up teaching of some sort – teaching that goes beyond the requirements of the actual debriefing. Indeed, some exercises may serve as a 'jumping-off point' for an extended series of lessons, or for other forms of study by the participants. Such follow-up study might take the form of detailed investigations of specific issues raised by the exercise, carried out either by individuals or by groups. It might also take the form of a 'whole-class' activity of some sort, eg the preparation of a large model or a major display.

Detailed case study: how to run *North Sea Auction* with a class

We will now put the above guidelines on how to run a game or simulation with a class into context by providing detailed instructions on how to run one well-proven exercise – *North Sea Auction*. This is an extremely versatile simulation/game that is designed to introduce pupils to the process by which oil companies compete for offshore oil concessions, explore them to see if they contain oil, and appraise any oilfields that they find. It can be used with pupils of all ages from roughly 8 upwards, and is equally suitable for use with college and university students. It is also the exercise that was used to introduce the class teachers who would be taking part in the 1990–91 Grampian Primary Industry Project to classroom games and simulations. *North Sea Auction* is an ideal exercise for teachers who have not used educational games and simulations before to try out with their classes. The authors guarantee that it will work well provided that the instructions given below are followed.

North Sea Auction was originally developed by Henry Ellington and Eric Addinall as part of the *Ekofisk – One of a Kind* multiple-media educational library published by Phillips Petroleum in 1980 for use in schools and colleges. It was later also included in *Licensed to Drill*, a second multiple-media educational library incorporating both manual and computer-based exercises that was published by Phillips in 1985. The exercise is made available with grateful thanks to Phillips Petroleum.

Background information for organizers

Oil and gas fields can form in any large sedimentary basin where suitable conditions prevail. Since such basins are found both under areas that are currently dry land and under the seas of the continental shelf, it is possible to find oil and natural gas both onshore and offshore. Since the late 1960s, the continental shelf off the coast of Britain has proved to be a major province for the discovery of gas and oil fields. Many such fields have now been discovered and developed, and new ones are regularly being found.

Initially, the search for oil or gas involves identification of a sedimentary basin containing rocks of the type and age likely to contain trapped hydrocarbons. If the area being searched is one whose geological structure is not well known, such basins can be found by means of an aerial magnetometer survey. This measures the magnetic properties of the underlying bedrock, and thus enables any sedimentary basins to be identified and their overall extent determined.

Once a sedimentary basin has been found, the type of rocks it contains can be determined by carrying out a gravimetric survey, in which local variations in the Earth's gravitational field produced by strata of different thicknesses are measured. Finally, the detailed structure of the strata in the basin is determined by carrying out a seismic survey. Here, shock waves produced by a shot or explosion are sent into the strata, and the resulting reflections from the boundaries between the different layers are detected using microphones or hydrophones and analysed by computer. In this way, the positions of likely oil or gas fields are identified *before* any actual drilling takes place.

Once a sedimentary basin has been surveyed and the main features of its structure determined, the various companies who are involved in the offshore oil and gas industries compete for licences to carry out exploratory drilling in the most promising areas. The way in which the governments who control the different sectors of the North Sea allocate such licences shows considerable variation, but the method used in the British sector (see Figure 3.3) is the

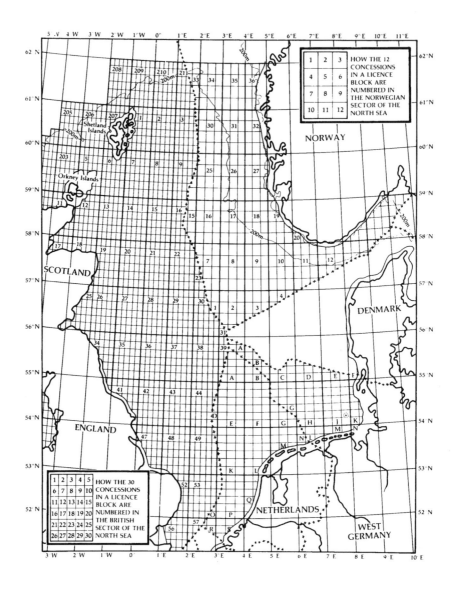

Figure 3.3 A map of the North Sea showing the different national sectors and how they are divided into licence blocks and concessions.

sealed-bid auction. Here, the British Government makes it known that certain specified areas in its sector are under offer, and the various interested companies submit confidential bids for any concessions in which they are interested by a specified date. Each concession is then allocated to the highest bidder when the bids are examined.

Once a company has acquired the rights to a concession, it generally carries out a further, very thorough seismic survey in order to determine the detailed structure of the strata that it contains. The company's geologists and geophysicists then use computers to collate the resulting data, and the results are interpreted to determine the most likely places where oil or gas may be found. The next crucial step is to drill a hole (or series of holes) into the strata to see whether the scientists were correct. Such exploratory wells are normally drilled using semi-submersible exploration rigs, which are towed into position by tugs and anchored in place while the drilling is being carried out.

If the exploratory drilling is successful, and oil or gas is found, further appraisal wells are drilled to determine the physical extent of the field, its likely recoverable reserves (the total amount of oil and gas that it would be technically feasible and economically viable to extract from the field), and the likely production rate. Only when this appraisal drilling has been completed will the company be able to decide whether or not it would be commercially worthwhile to develop the field.

How to run North Sea Auction

North Sea Auction is a simulation/game based on the process by which oil companies compete for offshore concessions, explore them for oil, and appraise any fields found. It can be used with any number of people from 12 to 60, and is ideal for use with a school class of roughly 20–30 people. Two versions of the exercise are available, one for use with younger pupils (aged roughly 8–12) and one for use with older pupils (aged 13 upwards) and adults. These differ in the way in which the 'auction' for concessions is organized, taking the form of a 'live' auction in the younger version and a 'sealed-bid' auction in the older version.

Both versions of the game are designed to help the participants to understand how the offshore oil industry operates, and to give them a feel for what it is like to work for an oil company. They are also designed to help them develop a wide range of useful process skills, including interpersonal skills, team skills, problem-solving skills and decision-making skills.

Preparatory work

To run the 'younger' version of the exercise, you will require sufficient copies of the map of the North Sea shown in Figure 3.3 to give every participant a

1	2	3	4	5
not at all promising	not at all promising	not at all promising	not at all promising	not at all promising
6	**7**	**8**	**9**	**10**
not at all promising	not very promising	quite promising	quite promising	not very promising
11	**12**	**13**	**14**	**15**
not very promising	quite promising	very promising	very promising	quite promising
16	**17**	**18**	**19**	**20**
quite promising	very promising	extremely promising	extremely promising	very promising
21	**22**	**23**	**24**	**25**
not very promising	quite promising	very promising	very promising	quite promising
26	**27**	**28**	**29**	**30**
not at all promising	not very promising	not very promising	not very promising	not at all promising

Figure 3.4 The schematic map of the licence block on offer for use in the 'younger' version of *North Sea Auction*.

1 not at all promising	2 not at all promising	3 not at all promising	4 not at all promising	5 not at all promising
6 not at all promising	7 not very promising	8 quite promising	9 quite promising	10 not very promising
11 not very promising	12 quite promising	13 very promising	14 very promising	15 quite promising
16 quite promising	17 very promising	18 extremely promising	19 extremely promising	20 very promising
21 not very promising	22 quite promising	23 very promising	24 very promising	25 quite promising
26 not at all promising	27 not very promising	28 not very promising	29 not very promising	30 not at all promising

Enter bids in space provided

Key to coding of concessions

Not at all promising: There is a very low probability of finding oil (1 in 6), and, if oil is found, the field will be small (see table below).

Not very promising: There is a low probability of finding oil (2 in 6), and, if oil is found, the field will be small-medium in size (see table below).

Quite promising: There is a reasonable probability of finding oil (3 in 6), and, if oil is found, the field will probably be medium-sized (see table below).

Very promising: There is a high probability of finding oil (4 in 6), and, if oil is found, the field is likely to be medium–large in size (see table below).

Extremely promising: There is a very high probability of finding oil (5 in 6), and, if oil is found there is a good chance that the field will be large or very large (see table below).

Likely sizes of fields in different concessions (assuming that oil is in fact found)

CODING OF CONCESSION					Size of field (recoverable
not at all promising	not very promising	quite promising	very promising	extremely promising	reserves in millions of barrels of oil)
3 in 6 chance	2 in 6 chance	1 in 6 chance			20
3 in 6 chance	2 in 6 chance	1 in 6 chance	1 in 6 chance		50
	2 in 6 chance	3 in 6 chance	1 in 6 chance	1 in 6 chance	120
		1 in 6 chance	3 in 6 chance	1 in 6 chance	300
			1 in 6 chance	3 in 6 chance	800
				1 in 6 chance	2000

Figure 3.5 The schematic map of the licence block on offer for use in the 'older' version of *North Sea Auction*.

1	2	3	4	5
6	7	8	9	10
11	12	13	14	15
16	17	18	19	20
21	22	23	24	25
26	27	28	29	30

Figure 3.6 The master for use in preparation of the OHP transparency of the plan of the licence block on offer.

copy. Run these off on A4 sheets using a photocopier with an enlargement facility. You will also require a similar number of copies of the schematic map of the licence block on offer shown in Figure 3.4. In addition, you will require a set of 'simulated money' for use in the live-auction phase of the game. Produce sufficient 'notes' to provide each competing team (between 4 and 6 in all) with a total of £100 million (or 100 million dollars, depending on the local currency); suggested denominations: 2 × £20 million; 4 × £10 million; 2 × £5 million; 10 × £1 million.

To run the 'older' version of the game, you will again require sufficient numbers of the map of the North Sea to give every participant a copy. You will also need sufficient numbers of the somewhat more detailed schematic map of the licence block on offer shown in Figure 3.5 to give each participant a copy, plus one extra copy for each competing team (for submitting their sealed auction bids). No simulated money is required in this case.

For both versions of the exercise, you will also need an OHP transparency of the plan of the licence block on offer shown in Figure 3.6, for use to display the names of the 'companies' who obtain the various concessions, to show whether they find oil, and to show the sizes of the resulting fields. Again, use a photocopier with an enlargement facility for this purpose, taking care to use an acetate sheet that will not melt in the photocopier. You will also require an overhead projector and screen, a set of coloured marker pens (medium tipped) and one standard 6-sided die, for use in the 'exploration' and 'appraisal' phases of the game.

Note that both versions of the game require roughly 40–60 minutes.

Before running the exercise (either version), you should carry out whatever preliminary teaching on the nature of oil and the oil industry that you consider appropriate.

Briefing the participants (both versions)
To start the exercise, divide the class into up to six competing teams, and assign each team the name of a major oil company (eg Shell, BP, Esso, Phillips, Mobil, Conoco). Issue each group with sufficient copies of the map of the North Sea to provide each participant with a copy. With younger pupils, also provide each group with copies of Figure 3.4 (one per participant) plus a set of simulated money (£100 million or 100 million dollars). With older pupils, provide each group with sufficient copies of Figure 3.5 for each participant to have their own copy, plus one extra copy per group (for submitting their sealed bids).

Now use Figure 3.3 to explain how the North Sea is divided into national sectors by median lines drawn midway between the shores of the bordering countries, and point out how this resulted in Britain receiving by far the largest sector. Explain how the British sector is divided into licence blocks

each 1 degree of latitude by one degree of longitude in area, and how each
licence block is divided into 30 concessions, numbered in the way shown in the
inset at the bottom left-hand corner of Figure 3.3. Outline the process by which
oil companies can bid for concessions by sealed-bid auction when a given
licence block is made available by the British Government, and explain that
one such block is being made available for the purpose of the game (do not say
which block it is, but indicate that it is 'somewhere west of the Shetlands').

Now refer the group to either Figure 3.4 or Figure 3.5 as appropriate, and
explain that this summarizes the findings of the preliminary magnetic,
gravimetric and seismic surveys that have been carried out so far. Point out
that the 30 concessions in the licence block have different probabilities of
containing oil, ranging from 1 in 6 for a 'not at all promising' concession to 5
in 6 for an 'extremely promising' concession. Also point out how the likely size
of any resulting field (in terms of its recoverable reserves in millions of barrels
of oil) also varies from concession to concession, as shown in the table at the
foot of Figure 3.5. In the case of a 'not at all promising' concession, for
example, the largest possible field is one with recoverable reserves of 50
million barrels; in the case of an 'extremely promising' concession, on the
other hand, there is a 1 in 6 chance of any resulting field turning out to be
another 'Forties' or 'Brent', with recoverable reserves of 2000 million barrels.

Finally, tell each team that they are responsible for bidding for concessions
on behalf of their respective 'companies'. Each team has up to £100 million
(or 100 million dollars) available for this purpose, which it can bid for the
various concessions in any way it likes, in bids of £1 million (1 million dollars)
or integral multiples thereof. It is up to the teams whether they spread their
bids over a large number of concessions or concentrate them on the most
promising concessions. They should, however, try to maximize their likely
return in terms of concessions acquired and total recoverable reserves
eventually discovered. With younger pupils, tell them that they will be taking
part in a 'live' auction rather than a sealed-bid auction, because this is 'more
fun'. With older pupils, tell them that they will be taking part in a sealed-bid
auction similar to the one that is carried out in real life, apart from the fact
that the 'real' auction has no upper limit on bids. In both cases, tell the pupils
that they will 'explore' their concessions and 'appraise' any fields found later
in the game.

The 'auction' phase of the game (younger version)

This should be done by displaying the OHP transparency of Figure 3.6 and
telling the teams that they have 5 minutes to plan their overall bidding
strategies (whether to concentrate their bids on the most promising
concessions, spread their bids over a larger number of concessions, or simply
bid for everything!). Then auction each of the 30 concessions in turn, allowing

bids of any size in multiples of £1 million (1 million dollars). Write the name of each successful 'company' in the top third of the concession displayed on the OHP after the auction of each has been completed, preferably using a different colour of marker pen for each team.

The 'auction' phase of the game (older version)

First, tell the teams that they have 15–25 minutes (depending on the time available) to decide on their bidding strategies and submit their sealed bids on their extra copy of Figure 3.5. Tell them to remember to write the name of their 'company' at the top of their bid sheet! Also, warn them that they will be disqualified from the auction if they break the rules (by failing to meet the deadline for submission of their bids, by exceeding the allowable bid total of 100 million pounds or dollars, or by submitting bids that are not integral multiples of 1 million pounds or dollars). Once the teams start work, check that they all understand the procedure and answer any specific questions that they may have. If you are not sure what answer to give to any such question, improvise; remember that *you* are in charge!

Once all the bids have been submitted, ask each team to send a representative to the front of the room to witness the scrutiny process and ensure that everything is done properly. Display the OHP transparency of the licence block, and work your way through the various concessions in numerical order, determining which team has acquired each. Print the name of the successful team in the top third of the concession in each case, again preferably using a different colour of marker pen for each team. In the event of tied bids for a given concession, ask the representatives of the teams involved to throw the die in turn, the one with the highest number being allocated the concession. If necessary, repeat the process until a winner emerges.

The 'exploration' phase of the game (both versions)

Once you have worked your way through all 30 concessions, ask each team to send a representative to the front of the room to participate in the 'exploration' process (a different representative in the case of the older pupils). Then work through the various concessions that have been acquired by 'oil companies', asking the representative of the 'company' that has acquired each concession to explore for oil by throwing the die. The numbers that indicate whether oil is present for the different types of concession are shown in Figure 3.7.

Once each concession has been 'explored', write 'OIL!' or 'NO OIL' in the middle third of the concession on the OHP transparency of the licence block.

Type of concession	Die numbers which indicate that oil is present	Die numbers which indicate that no oil is present
Not at all promising	6	5, 4, 3, 2, 1
Not very promising	6, 5	4, 3, 2, 1
Quite promising	6, 5, 4	3, 2, 1
Very promising	6, 5, 4, 3	2, 1
Extremely promising	6, 5, 4, 3, 2	1

Figure 3.7 The die numbers that indicate whether or not oil is present for the different types of concessions shown in Figures 3.4 and 3.5.

The 'appraisal' phase of the game (both versions)

Once all the assigned concessions have been explored, again ask each team to send a (different) representative to the front of the room to participate in the 'appraisal' process. Then work your way through the various concessions in which oil has been found, asking the representative of the operating 'company' to appraise the field by throwing the die. The numbers that indicate fields of different sizes for the different types of concession are shown in Figure 3.8.

Not at all promising	Not very promising	Quite promising	Very promising	Extremely promising	Size of field (millions of barrels)
1, 2, 3	1, 2	1			20
4, 5, 6	3, 4	2	1		50
	5, 6	3, 4, 5	2	1	120
		6	3, 4, 5	2	300
			6	3, 4, 5	800
				6	2000

Figure 3.8 The die numbers that indicate fields of different sizes for the different types of concessions shown in Figures 3.4 and 3.5.

Once each field has been 'appraised', write the size of the field (in millions of barrels of recoverable oil) in the bottom third of the concession on the OHP transparency of the licence block. Once all the fields have been appraised, determine the winning team by finding which has acquired the greatest total of recoverable reserves.

Debriefing the participants (both versions)

If time allows, debrief the participants by discussing the following matters, and any others that you consider appropriate.

- Why the winning team thinks it was successful; was it because of their brilliant bidding strategy, or simply due to good luck in throwing the die?
- Why the team with the lowest total reserves thinks it was unsuccessful; was it bad planning, or simply sheer bad luck?
- What the participants learned about teamwork from taking part in the exercise.
- What the participants learned about the need for good planning and good luck in high-risk activities such as the offshore oil industry.

Obviously, the depth of treatment should be greater when running the 'older' version of the game.

4

Using Games and Simulations with Nursery Classes

This is the first of four chapters which look in detail at how games and simulations can be used with pupils of different ages. It deals with their use at nursery level, ie with pre-school children of age roughly 3–5 who have yet to acquire basic literacy and numeracy.

Some basic features of nursery education

Throughout the world, the importance of 'nursery' or 'pre-school' education is becoming increasingly – albeit somewhat belatedly – recognized. In Britain, for example, it is now Government policy to make such education available to all children – not just to those who are fortunate enough to live in an area where the local authority provides some nursery classes, or whose parents can afford to pay for private pre-school education. It is now generally accepted that children who receive such education are placed at a considerable advantage over those whose formal education only starts when they enter primary school at the age of 5 or 6 – *after* they have completed the most formative years of their development, according to child psychologists.

Nursery education has always been an exciting and challenging area to work in, but the task of the teachers responsible for delivering it has often been made more difficult by an almost complete lack of central curricular direction. Since nursery education has traditionally been non-statutory, very few local authorities have felt it necessary to provide nursery staff with any form of overall strategic guidance as to the sort of curriculum they are expected to provide for their young charges, let alone any detailed advice on how to put the curriculum into practice. Head teachers have often got round this by looking at the current guidelines and prescribed curriculum for primary education, and trying to work towards the basic levels that P1 pupils are expected to achieve. In this way, it is possible to build some continuity into the growing child's early educational experience.

In order to help ensure that nursery education plays an effective role in preparing children for what will happen once they move on to primary school, the authors believe that it should incorporate the following core elements. First, it should help children to develop the listening and spoken-language skills that lay the foundations for the acquisition of basic literacy. Second, it should help them to develop all the various 'pre-maths skills' that lay similar foundations for the acquisition of basic numeracy. Third, it should increase their knowledge of and competence in important activities related to their everyday lives. Fourth, it should increase their knowledge and awareness of their environment. Fifth, it should help them to develop their social and interpersonal skills. Finally, it should help them to realize their innate creativity through things like the expressive arts. Wherever possible, nursery education should be *active* rather than passive, since pre-school children have a very short attention span (two or three minutes at most) and learn most effectively if they themselves are heavily involved in what is going on.

How games and simulations can contribute to nursery education

Games are key activities in most nursery schools and classes, but are not always properly integrated into the curriculum or used to achieve specific educational objectives. If this is the case, much of their potential educational value is wasted, since we have seen that games are very effective in helping to bring about worthwhile learning when the educational and gaming aspects are used to complement and reinforce one another. With very young children, games should have only a very few rules, and these should be both simple and easily understood. The games should involve *repetition* and *reinforcement* of key activities, and, wherever possible, should also relate directly to the children's own experience. Any associated materials should also be simple, should be as bright and colourful as possible, and should not rely on either written language or written numbers, since most nursery children have not yet acquired basic reading or number-recognition skills. Bearing these general guidelines in mind, however, it is possible to use classroom games and simulations in all of the key curricular areas identified in the last section. Let us now show how this can be done.

Developing listening and spoken-language skills

Listening skills are very hard to develop in the pre-school child, partly because of their very short attention span. For this reason, such skills have traditionally been developed through highly interactive whole-class or small-group teaching, with the pupils being asked questions or invited to contribute to the proceedings on an ongoing basis, or via short one-to-one sessions with the teacher or nursery nurse.

One useful technique that can be used to help nursery pupils to develop such listening skills is the *story-tape game*. Here, the teacher makes up a short story related to some activity that is likely to be of interest to the children – a visit to the seaside, for example, as part of the teaching of a particular theme such as 'the sea'. The story is structured round five or six key objects or concepts, and these are drawn on cards (see Figure 4.1). Note that these cards should be fairly large (10cm x 8cm, say) to make it easy for the children to handle them.

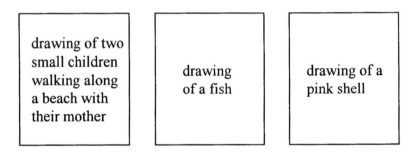

Figure 4.1 A sequence of cards for a story-tape game based on a visit to the seaside.

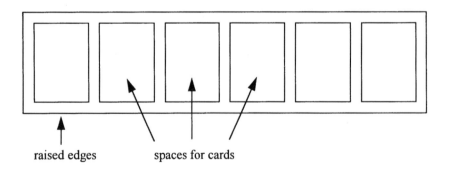

Figure 4.2 A board suitable for use in a six-picture story-tape game.

A linear 'board' with spaces into which the cards can be placed should also be prepared (see Figure 4.2).

Finally, the teacher records the story on a tape cassette, incorporating an attention-getting sound such as the ringing of a bell after the end of each section, followed by a pause. The latter should be long enough to enable the child listening to the tape to identify the picture card associated with the section and slot it into the correct space on the board, working from left to right (ten seconds should be more than enough). The start of the story of 'a visit to the seaside' might go as follows:

'Last Tuesday, Sarah and John went for a walk along the beach with their Mummy'. (*bell rings; pause*)
'In among the rocks, they found a pool with a big fish swimming in it'.
(*bell rings; pause*)
'Further along the beach, Sarah saw a beautiful pink shell, and picked it up'.
(*bell rings; pause*)

and so on

Story-tape games of this type can be based on virtually any topic, and can thus be built into the teaching of a wide range of themes. They can also form a stepped sequence, with the stories getting progressively longer, having more sections and having shorter pauses between the sections as the children develop their ability to listen, their powers of concentration and their manipulative skills. Games of this type can also be used to help children develop their memory, by asking them to tell the story to the teacher or nursery nurse once they have listened to the tape. They thus constitute an extremely versatile, powerful – and simple – aid to the development of a wide range of skills.

Listening skills can also be developed through simple computer games designed for use at nursery level, provided that these are based on *spoken* material rather than written material. Teachers who have access to the necessary equipment (basically, a computer with a built-in sound facility) and possess the necessary IT skills might like to try their hand at developing their own custom-designed games of this type. Alternatively, they can probably find something suitable for use with their pupils in one of the commercial software catalogues.

Developing pre-maths skills

Games and simulations are also ideal for developing the various shape-recognition, pattern-recognition, matching, positioning, sequencing and other skills that lay the foundations for the acquisition of basic numeracy and, later on, basic mathematical skills. Practically all the games and simulations described in this chapter develop skills of this general type to a greater or lesser extent, but some of the most useful are the various forms of *jigsaw*. Jigsaws are generally thought of as two dimensional, but a much simpler type – the so-called *linear jigsaw* – can prove extremely effective at pre-school and early-primary level. Such a linear jigsaw consists basically of a strip of card divided into a number of separate pieces in the way shown in Figure 4.3. Note how the shapes of the male and female sections that enable the pieces to interlock with one another are different for each junction.

Such linear jigsaws can be used simply as abstract shape-matching and sequencing exercises, and are also useful for developing pupils' manipulative and positioning skills. Their educational effectiveness is, however, greatly increased if they are provided with an appropriate representational content of some sort, preferably linked to some topic that the children have been studying in class. This content can be incorporated by drawing simple pictures representing the various stages of an ordered sequence or process on the various pieces, so that the child has to build up the required sequence by fitting the pieces of the jigsaw together. Figure 4.4, for example, shows a linear jigsaw that represents the various stages in the procedure by which an offshore oil installation is evacuated following an explosion or fire – a game that was developed by Monica Gordon as part of the project that she ran at York Street Nursery School in connection with the 1990–91 Grampian Primary Industry Project (see the detailed case study at the end of the chapter for further information).

Conventional two-dimensional jigsaws can also be used extremely effectively at nursery level. These can be produced simply by cutting up a drawing or picture on a rectangular card into a number of pieces, and asking

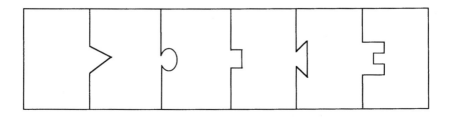

Figure 4.3 The structure of a typical linear jigsaw.

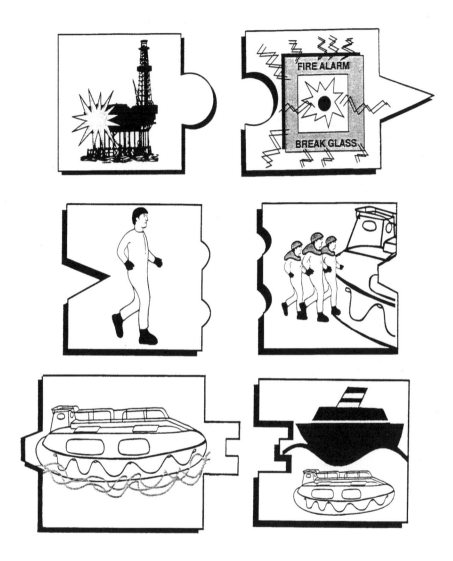

Figure 4.4 The *Rescue* linear jigsaw developed at York Street Nursery School in connection with the 1990–91 Grampian Primary Industry Project.

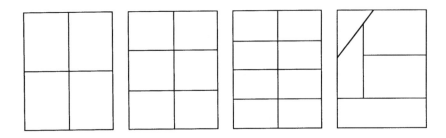

Figure 4.5 Progressively more difficult versions of a simple jigsaw.

the children to fit the pieces together again. Such jigsaws can be made progressively more demanding as the pupils develop their matching and pattern-building skills, some of the possible patterns of pieces in such a stepped sequence of games being shown in Figure 4.5. The degree of difficulty can also be varied by showing (or not showing) the children what the finished picture looks like.

Pre-maths skills of all types can, of course, also be developed via appropriate computer-based exercises. Again, those teachers with the necessary equipment and skills might like to try to develop their own. Others can simply see what is available commercially!

Increasing children's knowledge of important activities

Games and simulations can also be used at nursery level to increase children's knowledge and understanding of a wide range of important activities related to their everyday lives and their experience outside the school. They can, for example, be used to show children the correct order in which they should put on their various items of clothing when they are getting dressed in the morning. One way of doing this is by making use of simple *dressing-figure games*, in which they have to 'dress' a cardboard outline figure by adding various items of clothing in the correct order. Such games can be organized in a number of different ways, and can be played either by individual pupils or by small groups.

A good example of a game of this type is *Dressing the Lifeboatman*, another of the games developed by Monica Gordon in connection with her 1990–91 Grampian Primary Industry Project (again, see the detailed case study at the end of the chapter). This involved dressing the 'lifeboatman' in his protective clothing – his over-trousers, wellington boots, over-jacket, life-jacket, safety helmet and safety gloves (see Figure 4.6).

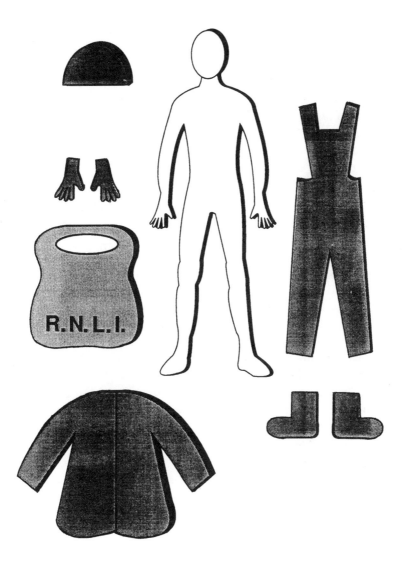

Figure 4.6 The various items used in *Dressing the Lifeboatman*.

The game was played by groups of up to four pupils, each of whom was given their own separate 'lifeboatman' and set of clothing. The players then took turns to throw a special six-sided die with different colours on its faces rather than the usual numbers. These different colours corresponded to coloured patches on the six items of clothing, with each child being able to add the appropriate item to his or her figure when its particular colour came up. The first player to complete dressing his or her 'lifeboatman' was the winner.

One interesting feature of the game is that it could be played at two levels – one fairly easy, one much more difficult. In the 'easy' version, the items of clothing could be added to the figure in any order. In the 'difficult' version, they had to be added in the *correct* order. This meant that the players not only had to remember what the 'correct' order was, but also had to wait patiently until the colour corresponding to the next item in the dressing sequence came up. The pupils had to be supervised by the teacher or nursery nurse until they mastered this version of the game, which was considerably more demanding than the 'easy' version, but also helped them to develop much higher-level skills.

Increasing children's knowledge of their environment

Helping children to become aware of, make sense of and cope with their environment is one of the most important functions of nursery education. Practically all the different types of game described so far could be used for this purpose, another extremely useful type being those that involve matching pictures or images that relate to their experience of some aspect of their environment. Games based on the *lotto* paradigm, in which the pupils have to collect cards carrying the specific set of pictures shown on their own particular 'board', are one form of this. This particular type of game will be dealt with in some detail later in this chapter and in Chapters 5 and 9, so we will not discuss it any further here. Games based on the *dominoes* paradigm, in which the pupils have to get rid of all their own pieces by adding them to a sequence built up on the table by matching one of the images shown at either end of the sequence, are another example of the genre.

Classroom 'picture-dominoes' games can be made as simple or as complicated as the teacher thinks appropriate. The simplest version that makes any real demands on the playing ability of the pupils involves preparing nine dominoes, each of which bears two images drawn from an overall set of six. If the game is to be used to reinforce the children's experience of some aspect of their environment – such as a visit to the supermarket – the six images could represent different things that can be purchased in a supermarket or different aspects of the 'shopping experience' (pushing the trolley, taking items from the shelves, going through the checkout, and so on). Alternatively, they could represent a combination of the two, as in the set of possible dominoes shown in Figure 4.7.

A set of dominoes of this type would be used by two competing players. The dominoes would be placed face down, shuffled, and each player would pick four, taking turns to pick them. The remaining domino would then be

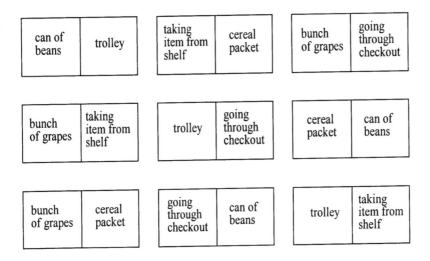

Figure 4.7 A possible set of dominoes based on a 'supermarket' theme.

turned over, and the first player to place one of his or her dominoes alongside it would start the game. Play would then continue as in 'conventional' dominoes, with the players taking turns to lay down a piece that matches the previous picture and missing their turn if unable to do so. The first player to get rid of all his or her dominoes would be the winner.

In addition to reinforcing the pupils' experience of some aspect of their environment, a game of this type can help them to develop their pre-maths and manipulative skills. It can also serve as a useful vehicle for helping them to develop their social and interpersonal skills. Clearly, computer games and simulations could again be used for similar purposes.

Developing social and interpersonal skills

The nursery school is the place where many children start to develop the basic social and interpersonal skills that are such an important feature of early education. Any game or simulation that puts them in a situation where they have to interact with their fellow pupils plays a useful role in helping them to develop these skills.

One game that Monica Gordon has found particularly useful in this role is *Setting the Table*. This is designed for four players, and involves the use of four 'trays' made of different colours of card (red, blue, green and yellow), with outlines marked showing where the various pieces of cutlery and other items should be placed. There are four sets of these various items (knife; fork; spoon; glass; plate; napkin) on shaped cards, again coloured red, blue, green and yellow. There is also a special large die, with drawings of the various items on its six faces.

To play the game, the children take turns to throw the die, picking up the item indicated and placing it on their tray if they have not already done so. The winner is the first player to complete his or her tray. As well as helping them to develop their social skills (learning to take their turn to play, learning to be patient when waiting for the appropriate symbols to appear, and so on), the game is also a useful vehicle for developing a wide range of other skills (colour recognition, matching skills, placing skills, etc). It has been found to be particularly useful with 'all-day' nursery classes where lunch is served, in extending 'house play', and in teaching about situations like setting up a cafe.

Fostering creative expression

Games and simulations also provide ideal vehicles for children to develop their innate creative powers and artistic self-expression. Role-playing simulations are particularly useful in this regard, enabling the participants to act out a variety of situations that provide ample scope for such creativity and self-expression. The traditional 'play house' is a good example of a simulation of this type, and the imaginative teacher should have no difficulty in thinking of many other simulated situations from which their pupils can benefit. As the pupils develop and mature, these situations can be made progressively more realistic and demanding. They are, of course, also ideal for helping pupils to develop their spoken-language, interpersonal and social skills, and for learning about their environment.

Detailed case study

Let us now end this chapter by taking a detailed look at how games and simulations were built into a major curriculum-development project in one particular school – York Street Nursery School in Aberdeen. This was the only nursery school to take part in the 1990–91 Grampian Primary Industry Project, a region-wide initiative designed to increase pupils' knowledge and understanding of the business side of industry through the medium of games and simulations and the formation of school–industry links.

York Street Nursery School (which has since closed down) was a small school, with 40 pupils divided into two classes. At the time, it had two teachers (the Head Teacher, Monica Gordon, and Valerie Kennedy) plus three nursery nurses (all British nursery schools employ such nursery nurses to help the teachers look after their pupils). The school was located right in the centre of Aberdeen's harbour area, and already had a long tradition of involvement in harbour-related activities through visits by pupils to the harbour and visits to the school by various people who worked there, including the crew of the Aberdeen lifeboat. It was therefore not really surprising that Monica Gordon chose 'life-saving at sea' as the theme for her school project, since the environment in which the school was located provided a rich source of experiences and case studies that could be used to support such a project.

In tackling the project, the staff built on their already excellent working relationship with the crew of the Aberdeen lifeboat by forming links with several other organizations involved in the work of Aberdeen harbour and the offshore oil industry that generates a large proportion of its activities. These included RGIT Survival Ltd (a commercial unit of the Robert Gordon University that provides safety training for offshore personnel), Aberdeen Fire Service, Aberdeen City Police Community Service, Hamilton Brothers Oil Company, and York Street Industrial Training Centre. Staff of all these various organizations became enthusiastically involved in the work of the project, coming to the school to give talks, show videos, demonstrate equipment, and so on, and also arranging for the pupils to visit their own establishments. They also helped the school to build up its own collection of offshore-rescue-related equipment and materials, including a large model of an offshore oil rig, models of rescue boats and helicopters, water tanks in which the pupils could carry out experiments on the movement of boats, floating, sinking, etc and a library of books, photographs, videos, puzzles and other materials designed to enrich the pupils' learning. Figure 4.8 shows the local Community Policeman working with the pupils during one of his visits, and clearly enjoying the experience just as much as the children!

In connection with the project, Mrs Gordon and Mrs Kennedy developed several games and simulations that were directly related to the theme of offshore rescue. The first of these was the *Rescue* linear jigsaw shown in Figure 4.4. This was a simple pattern-building simulation/game based on the sequence of events during an emergency on an offshore oil installation, showing the various stages in the ensuing evacuation. The six illustrations of these various stages had to be fitted together in the correct order, with the children playing the game either singly or in pairs. The main educational purpose of the game was to reinforce the children's knowledge of the evacuation procedure on an offshore installation, and place a topic of which they already had direct experience (offshore survival craft) into its proper context. It also helped the children to develop pre-reading and pre-maths skills, spoken-language skills, left-to-right sequencing skills, hand–eye coordination and fine-motor skills. In the opinion of Mrs Gordon, this was

Figure 4.8 The local Community Policeman working with pupils of York Street Nursery School during the Grampian Primary Industry Project.

probably the game that was *most* relevant to the project as a whole, since it helped the children to relate the offshore safety craft that they had studied in class, visited, and watched entering and leaving the harbour to the actual role that they are designed for – saving people's lives during an emergency. It is an excellent example of a classroom game in which the educational and gaming elements are extremely well integrated.

The second game that was developed specially for use in the project was the *Dressing the Lifeboatman* simulation/game that was described earlier in this chapter and is illustrated in Figure 4.6. As we saw, this was a simple 'dressing' game in which groups of four children competed to be the first to complete dressing their own particular 'lifeboatman' (an outline cardboard figure) in his protective equipment. It was designed to reinforce the children's knowledge of the dressing process (parts of the body; the various items of clothing and where they are worn; the correct dressing sequence, and so on) in a context that related directly to the theme of the project on which they were working (offshore rescue). It also helped to reinforce their knowledge and understanding of the process by which they themselves got dressed in the morning. The game also helped to develop a wide range of other skills, including social and interpersonal skills, hand–eye coordination and 'placing' skills, and spoken-language skills. The more advanced version of the game (in which the various items of clothing had to be placed on the figure in the correct order) also helped the children to develop their memory – something that is very important for very young children, since it is their *only* way of storing information until they acquire basic literacy and numeracy.

The third game developed for use in the project was a 'picture-lotto' game based on features of the North Sea and harbour environment that the children had come across in connection with their work on the 'life-saving at sea' project (see Figure 4.9). It was designed for 2–6 players, each of which was given a lotto board containing six colour-coded illustrations representing things like a life-jacket, a supply boat, an offshore oil platform, a lighthouse, and so on. A set of cards (also colour-coded) representing the various illustrations was shuffled and placed face down in a single pile. The children then took turns to turn over the top card and place it on their own board if it matched a vacant space. The winner was the first player to fill all six places.

Figure 4.9 The picture-lotto game developed for use in York Street Nursery School's work on the Grampian Primary Industry Project.

The game was designed to reinforce the children's knowledge and recognition of things they had seen in and around Aberdeen harbour during outings and visits, or had learned about in class during their work on the project. It again also helped to develop a wide range of other useful skills, including social and interpersonal skills, pre-maths and pre-reading skills, spoken-language skills and manipulative and placing skills. Picture-lotto games of this type are one of the most useful tools available to the nursery teacher, since they can be used in the teaching of virtually any topic, and do not rely on the children's ability to read.

Taken overall, Monica Gordon and her staff adjudged their Grampian Primary Industry Project work to have been a resounding success, helping the children to develop knowledge and skills that covered all the key areas of the nursery curriculum identified at the beginning of this chapter. They also felt that the use of classroom games and simulations had made a very significant contribution to this success, and, as a result, became even more firmly convinced of the great educational value of exercises of this type. The authors hope that the work described will help to encourage other nursery teachers to make similar use of custom-designed educational games with their own classes. If they wish to do so, they will find detailed guidance on how to design their own games in Chapters 8 and 9.

5

Using Games and Simulations with Early-Primary Pupils

This is the second of the four chapters that look in detail at how games and simulations can be used with pupils of different ages. It deals with their use at early-primary level, ie with pupils of age roughly 5–8 who are undergoing the first stages of their statutory education.

Some basic features of early-primary education

The early years of primary education are in many ways the most important stage of a child's compulsory education. These are the 'make or break' years in which pupils are expected to develop the basic literacy and numeracy skills that lay the foundations for everything else that follows. If they succeed in acquiring these key skills at this stage, the remainder of their primary and secondary education generally proceeds fairly smoothly, and prepares them to move on to the post-compulsory educational opportunities of which more and more of our future citizens are now availing themselves. If they do *not* acquire basic reading, writing and number skills at this stage, however, they tend to spend the rest of their primary and secondary education trying to catch up with their more fortunate peers, and, in many cases, never manage to do so.

In many ways, early-primary education is a continuation of the nursery education that was described in the previous chapter. In primary schools, however, teachers are given considerably greater guidance regarding the *strategic direction* of the curriculum they are required to deliver, the *specific targets* they should be aiming to achieve at each stage, and the *teaching methods* that they should employ in order to attain these targets. Although such guidelines vary in detail from country to country and from one local education authority to another, they all tend to include the following key elements. First, they all stress the vital importance of developing basic spoken-language, reading and writing skills, together with basic number, computational and (increasingly) IT skills. As we have seen, these are the core skills on which everything else depends. They also stress the importance of developing detailed knowledge of specific activities that play a key part in the children's everyday lives, of increasing their knowledge and awareness of their environment, of laying the foundations of social and – in Britain – religious awareness (religious education is a statutory part of the curriculum in British schools), and of helping pupils to develop their creativity and powers of artistic expression. Class teachers are encouraged to integrate these various elements into a cohesive, well-balanced curriculum, making appropriate use of whole-class teaching, individual work and group work. In many local authorities, they are encouraged to do so by building their teaching round a series of overall 'themes' that provide pupils with the opportunity to develop the different types of knowledge and skill listed.

How games and simulations can contribute to early-primary education

The authors have found that classroom games and simulations are capable of making a very significant contribution to the teaching of all the key areas of the early-primary curriculum. As with the games that are used at nursery level, it is important that the educational and gaming elements should be well integrated, and it is also important that the rules should be as simple and clear as possible. With the very youngest pupils, who have yet to acquire basic reading and number-recognition skills, the associated materials should again be free of written language and number, but these can gradually be phased in as the children's reading and number skills improve. Indeed, as we will see, games and simulations can be used to help them develop these skills. It is again important that classroom games and simulations should involve repetition and reinforcement of key activities and should relate to the children's own experience as much as possible. Let us now see how such exercises can be used to help achieve the different types of educational objectives that were identified in the last section.

Developing language skills

Children come to primary school with a wide range of language skills. Those who have been to nursery school, or whose parents have taken the trouble to help them develop such skills, will be able to communicate fairly effectively and confidently and will have a reasonable vocabulary. Others will barely be able to communicate at all, and will have a very limited vocabulary. Indeed, many children entering primary school will have picked up what little vocabulary they have mainly from watching television! Games and simulations are ideal vehicles for helping children to develop their powers of spoken conversation, since they place them in non-threatening, supportive situations in which they are encouraged to interact with their peers. Such games can be designed to challenge the children, but to do so in such a way that success is always achieved (albeit with adult help in some cases). Such success builds upon itself, especially when reinforced by praise from the teacher, and steadily helps to increase the self-confidence of the pupils.

Helping children to develop their listening skills and increase their powers of concentration is a very important aspect of such early-language development, and is an area where well-designed classroom games can play a particularly important role. Story-tape games of the type described in the last chapter can be used equally effectively with very young primary pupils, as can picture-matching games of the *dominoes* and *lotto* type. Lotto games are particularly useful for developing listening skills if the teacher records the material that the children use to select the pictures on tape, so that a child can play the game over and over again until the material is mastered. Such games can be based on any topic, such as 'people who help us around the school'. A stepped game of this type might be based on a blank nine-squared lotto board of the type shown in Figure 5.1, together with three different sets of nine cards designed to fit on the board, sets that can be used by children who are at different stages of development.

The cards designed for use at level 1 would carry pictures of the different people who 'help us around the school' – eg the teacher, janitor, cook, school nurse, lollipop person, cleaner, community police representative, bus driver, and so on. The level 2 cards would carry both pictures of the various people and their descriptive names ('teacher', 'janitor', etc). The level 3 cards would only carry the descriptive names. The tape would contain short descriptions of the various people, with each description being followed by the ringing of a bell and a pause, so that the children can find the appropriate card and place it on the board. Such a game could be played both by groups of children and by individuals.

As we have seen, listening-lotto games of this type can be based on any topic and can be pitched at a number of different levels. With very young children, the nine-squared boards can be left completely blank, since the main object of the game is simply to identify all the cards being described and collect a complete set. With older children, the square on which each card has to be placed might be identified, eg by an appropriate word or symbol. This would make the game somewhat more demanding, but would also help develop a wider range of skills.

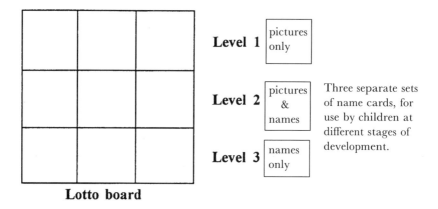

Figure 5.1 A stepped *listening-lotto* game for early-primary use.

Linear jigsaws of the type described in Chapter 4 can also be used to help children to develop their language skills. Such a jigsaw could be based on a topic such as 'a walk in the park', and could include as many pieces as the teacher felt necessary, with the number increasing with the age of the pupils. With very young pupils, the pieces could be made interlocking, as shown in Figure 5.2. With older children, simple cards could be used to make up the sequence.

The ways in which such linear jigsaws are used can also be varied according to the stage of development of the pupils. With very young children, simply building up the sequence and telling a simple story based on it might be sufficient. With slightly older children, matching sets of simple word cards, using known vocabulary, could be placed under the pictures, thus helping the children to write a story based on the sequence and encouraging the start of 'creative writing'. With even older children, who have developed the ability to write, they could be asked to write their own story based on the sequence, thus further encouraging the development of creative writing.

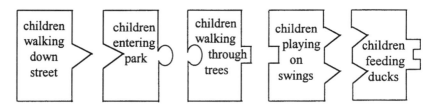

Figure 5.2 A linear jigsaw based on 'a walk in the park'.

READING PACK 1: Age 5-8

Cassette:£9.95   Disc:£12.95
Atari/Amiga/PC   Disc:£14.95

BBC/MASTER/COMPACT
*ARCHIMEDES   ELECTRON
AMIGA AMSTRAD CPC ATARI ST/E
COMMODORE 64 PC SPECTRUM/+3

* Archimedes version only available as part of "Bumper Pack 1"
(see end of catalogue)

Game 1:"Splashdown"
(Word building with simple letter
sounds)
In an exciting air-sea battle. up to 4
players have to type suitable letters to
complete their "word boats" (3 letter
words with 1st. 2nd or 3rd letter missing).

Game 2:"Firefight"
Consonant blends:
(sl,sm,sn,sp,st,sw,bl,br,cl,cr,dr,
dw,fl,fl,gr,pl,pr,tr,tw)
A player has to rescue the heroine from
the top of a burning building. by choosing
the right letter pairs to bridge the burning
holes in the words.

"Children really do like playing this game. They certainly see it
as a game, although there is reading involved. The graphics are
superb ...teachers found the different levels that could be set
and the range of letter pairs available allowed them to use
Firefight with a whole range of children over a period of time.
Without a doubt, this is a very good example of a computer
based reading game."
- EDUCATIONAL COMPUTING

NATIONAL CURRICULUM KEY STAGES 1 & 2
ATTAINMENT TARGETS: ENGLISH 2,4

Figure 5.3 The publicity material on two typical 'early reading' computer
games.

A whole range of *computer games* designed to help children to develop basic reading and writing skills are also available for use at early-primary level. Figure 5.3 shows the publicity material for two typical games of this type that are available from the HS Software Catalogue – one of the catalogues that is currently circulated to British schools. As can be seen, the games are carefully designed to fit in with specific stages of the English National Curriculum. Teachers wishing to use games of this type with their pupils are advised to use such catalogues to see what sort of exercises are available in their own countries, taking care to ensure that they can be used on the computers that they have at their disposal.

Developing pre-maths and number skills

As we saw in Chapter 4, games and simulations are ideal for helping very young children to develop all the various 'pre-maths skills' – shape-recognition, pattern-recognition, matching, sequencing, and so on – that lay the foundations for the development of basic numeracy. Linear jigsaws of the type shown in Figures 4.3, 4.4 and 5.2 are excellent for this purpose, as are 'two-dimensional' jigsaws of the type shown in Figure 4.5. Picture-matching games such as the various dominoes and lotto type games shown in Figures 4.7, 4.9 and 5.1 can also be used to develop such skills, as can many simple computer games (see Figure 5.4). Figure 5.5 shows the publicity material for a typical suite of early-maths computer games, again from the HS Software Catalogue. As can be seen, this is again designed to help pupils attain specific targets that form part of the English National Curriculum. Teachers wishing

Figure 5.4 Pupils using a computer game to develop their basic number skills.

MATHS PACK 1: Age 5-7
Cassette:N/A   Disc:£12.95

BBC/MASTER/COMPACT
ARCHIMEDES

"Maths Pack 1" is a totally new concept in educational software, and has been specifically designed to meet the demands of the National Curriculum:

* Wide range of options so that games can be adjusted to meet all ability levels, and to suit each child's individual rate of progress.
* Includes Matching (easy and difficult), Counting (forwards and backwards) and Sequencing numbers to 10.
* Unique disc record of a child's successes and errors for every game played !
* Program disc holds data for up to 36 children.
* Individual Scores screen gives detailed graphs of each child's progress.
* Summary Scores screen gives graphs of all children's scores on one screen.
* Program for printing score screens (Epson compatible printers only)
* User-friendly "Teacher" program for adding, altering and deleting childrens' names.
* Comprehensive user manual.

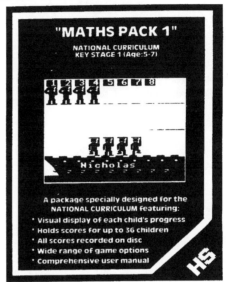

"MATHS PACK 1"

NATIONAL CURRICULUM
KEY STAGE 1 (Age:5-7)

Nicholas

A package specially designed for the
NATIONAL CURRICULUM featuring:
* Visual display of each child's progress
* Holds scores for up to 36 children
* All scores recorded on disc
* Wide range of game options
* Comprehensive user manual

HS

The fully enhanced Archimedes version of Maths Pack 1 features full W.I.M.P. control, digitised 256 colour animated graphics, together with sampled speech and sound effects!

"All these games have sensible options to make them suitable for children of any ability within the suggested age range....Pupil appeal, plus a record keeping system, mean that HS have a sure fire winner."-MICRO USER

NATIONAL CURRICULUM KEY STAGE 1
ATTAINMENT TARGETS: MATHS 2,4

Figure 5.5 The publicity material for a typical 'early maths' software package.

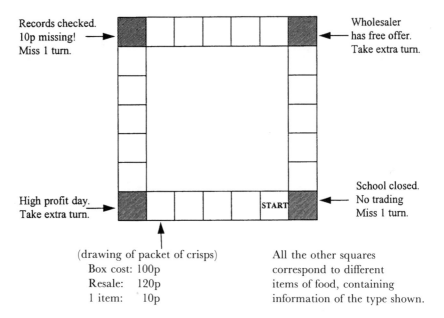

Figure 5.6 The basic features of the *Class Tuck Shop Game*.

to use games of this type with their own pupils should again consult the latest catalogues to see what is available.

Games and simulations can also be used extremely effectively to help pupils apply their basic number skills in situations that relate to their everyday experience. A good example of such a game is the *Class Tuck Shop Game*, designed for use in connection with theme teaching on the general topics of 'food' and 'shopping'. To play this particular game effectively, pupils should have developed basic number-recognition and counting skills, and should be familiar with the shopping process, reinforced, if possible, by a visit to a local food store or supermarket and by using the school 'tuck shop'.

As can be seen from Figure 5.6, the game is based on the *Monopoly* principle, but has a much simpler board than the original. Most of the squares correspond to different items of food – some expensive; some cheap – carrying information of the type shown. Cards carrying the information on these squares are available, as are sets of simulated money for use by the children. In the version designed for use in British schools, each child would be provided with, say, £10 in small notes, and the 'Bank' would hold a further supply. Each player (up to 6) would also be provided with their own special playing token.

The game is played in the same way as conventional *Monopoly*, movement round the board being controlled by taking turns to throw a single conventional numbered die. The object of the game is to make a profit from the operation of one's own 'tuck shop'. A player has the option of 'bulk buying' the item of food shown on a given square when landing on the square, and has to make a decision whether to do so or not. Once a player 'owns' a particular square, anyone else landing on it must *either* buy the whole box of items from the owner at the 'resale' price *or* pay a 'fine' corresponding to the cost of purchasing a single item. The game is generally played for an agreed period, at the end of which the player who has made the greatest profit is the winner.

In addition to providing an ideal vehicle for reinforcing the children's knowledge and understanding of numbers, basic counting and money handling, the *Class Tuck Shop Game* helps them to develop a wide range of other useful skills. These include reading skills, spoken-language skills, social skills and decision-making skills. It also helps to improve their knowledge of their environment.

Increasing children's knowledge of important activities

As at nursery level, children's knowledge and understanding of important activities related to their everyday lives can be increased by the use of classroom games and simulations. The *Class Tuck Shop Game* described above is one good example of an exercise of this type, since it not only helps the players to develop a wide range of useful skills but also helps them to learn about shopping for food, about the basic principles of trading, and about the importance of 'profit' in such trading. As we have seen, the game could be used in connection with the teaching of the general themes of 'food' or 'shopping'.

Another game that could be used in connection with the teaching of the 'food' theme is *Baking Happy Families*. This is based on the 'Happy Families' paradigm – one of the most useful models on which classroom games can be based, particularly at primary level (see Chapter 9). Such a game might be used as a follow-up to home-economics work in which the children learn how to bake different types of cake and biscuit, and would involve 'collecting the recipes' for making these different items.

A possible pack of cards for use in a game of this type might consist of six sets of five cards, each representing the various stages in the baking of the item in question. For use in British schools, the six items might be scones, pancakes, fairy cakes, jam tarts, melting moments and chocolate crispies (no doubt readers from other countries can think of their own such lists). For each item, a set of five cards would be prepared, colour-coded round the edges to facilitate easy recognition and carrying the name of the item (in small print) at the top. The cards would carry the information shown in Figure 5.7.

To play the game, the pack of 30 cards is shuffled, and the complete pack is

Picture of item	List of materials needed to make item	List of equipment needed to make item	Instructions on how to prepare item for baking	Instructions on how to bake item (cooking time, temperature)

Figure 5.7 The information on a set of *Baking Happy Families* cards.

dealt out to the players (up to six). Players then take turns to ask one of the other players for a particular card, having to remember to say 'please' as they do so, otherwise they lose their turn. If the other player holds the card requested, it has to be handed over, but, if the first player does not remember to say 'thank you', it has to be handed back and the offending player again loses their turn. Play continues until someone wins by collecting all the cards in a given set. When played in the way described, *Baking Happy Families* is also a good vehicle for developing social skills, as well as for helping pupils to develop their memory.

Increasing pupils' knowledge of their environment

Games and simulations are also extremely useful in helping young children develop awareness of and make sense of their environment. All sorts of different exercises can be used for this purpose, including linear jigsaws and 'picture-matching' games of the lotto, dominoes and snap type. All young children know how to play snap, so this is a particularly useful model on which to base classroom games. Snap-type games can again be based on virtually any topic. When teaching children about their environment, for example, such games can be based on the various types of trees, flowers, birds, animals etc that the children see around them or come across when they visit the countryside.

A game based on 'flowers', for example, might involve using a pack of 40 cards containing four each of ten different pictures of well-known flowers (in Britain, these might be 'pansies', 'snowdrops', 'crocuses', 'daffodils', 'tulips', 'poppies', 'lupins', 'roses', 'primroses' and 'bluebells'). For very young children, the cards would only carry pictures of the flowers, preferably brightly coloured. With slightly older children, they could carry both pictures of the flowers and their names. With even older children, there could also be a pack of cards carrying only the names of the flowers, to which they could progress once they had played the 'picture-and-names' version a few times. Use of such a stepped game would clearly help pupils to develop their reading skills and build up their vocabulary as well as reinforcing their knowledge of their environment.

One aspect of their environment with which it is essential that young children become familiar at the earliest possible age is *road safety*. Many different types of games and simulations can be used to help them develop the required knowledge and attitudes, a good example being the *Road Safety Ludo* game shown in Figure 5.8.

The game is based on conventional Ludo. The object is for the players to move their coloured playing tokens (one, two or three depending on the age of the pupils) from their individual 'start' circles to their individual 'finish' circles on the other side of the 'road' that runs round the 'finish' area of the board. They do this by moving each of their tokens once round the perimeter of the board in a clockwise direction, then in towards the centre, along their own coloured circles. Movement is controlled by throwing a single standard die.

The 'road-safety' element is built into the game through two packs of cards – 12 'question' (?) cards and 12 'chance' (C) cards. The 'questions' pack contains simple questions about road safety, based on what the pupils have been taught in class (eg 'How would you recognize a zebra crossing?'). The 'chance' pack contains eight 'good' cards (eg 'Well done! You crossed the

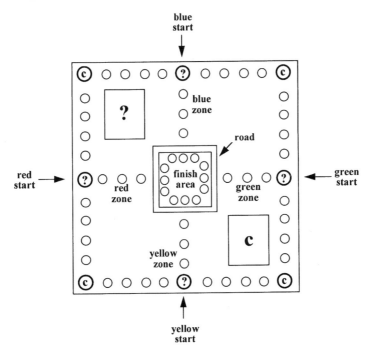

Figure 5.8 The board for the *Road Safety Ludo* game.

road safely! Take an extra turn) and four 'bad' cards (eg 'Oh dear! You forgot to look both ways before crossing! Move back three places). The two packs are placed face down in their respective boxes on the board. Players have to pick up a 'chance' card every time they land on a 'C' circle. They have to answer the question on the top 'question' card every time they land on a '?' circle *and* before they cross the 'road' into the 'finish' area. In each case, they are only allowed to move on if they answer the question correctly (the game is supervised by an adult, who decides whether each answer is correct, and, if not, explains why). If they do not answer the question correctly, they try the next question on their next turn, continuing in this way until they get a question right.

This is another good example of a game in which the 'gaming' and 'educational' factors are extremely well integrated. Its main object is to reinforce the children's knowledge of what constitutes 'good' road-safety practice, and to show them how important it is to follow whatever road-safety code they have been taught in class. It also helps them to practise simple number-recognition and counting skills, develop their reading skills, and develop their interpersonal and social skills. The game can be used with children of different ages by varying the number of counters used, by varying the reading age of the material on the cards, and by varying the amount of help given by the supervising adult.

Developing social and religious awareness

Classroom games and simulations can help children develop interpersonal and social skills of all types. When they involve groups of children, such exercises help them to develop their spoken-language skills, and encourage them to communicate and interact effectively with their peers. They also introduce them to some of the social conventions with which they will have to learn to comply in later life – not interrupting when other people are speaking, waiting for their turn, not losing their temper when things go badly, and so on. Many of the games described earlier in this chapter – lotto- and dominoes-based games, the *Class Tuck Shop Game*, *Baking Happy Families* and *Road Safety Ludo*, all help to develop such interpersonal skills and social awareness. No doubt readers can think of ideas for classroom activities that are specifically designed to achieve such objectives – role-playing simulations of different social situations, for example.

Games and simulations can also play an extremely useful role in religious education. In Britain, such education is a statutory part of the school curriculum, so all primary and secondary schools have to teach some form of 'RE'. At early-primary level, linear jigsaws of the type discussed earlier in this chapter are ideal vehicles for reinforcing religious teaching of all types. They can, for example, be used to make children more familiar with important episodes in the lives of Jesus, Mohammed, Buddha, Krishna and the other great prophets and religious leaders. A series of such linear jigsaws could deal with different aspects of the Christmas story, for example, covering such episodes as the journey to Bethlehem, the visit of the shepherds and the visit of the three kings. Such games could again be made progressively more demanding as the children's reading and writing skills develop and, with older pupils, could be used to help them develop their own story-telling and creative-writing skills. Teachers might like to think how they could use such games with their own pupils.

Lotto games can also prove extremely useful as vehicles for reinforcing religious teaching, and to help pupils get a feel for what life was like at the time when well-known religious figures lived. One useful game of this type is *Biblical Times Lotto*, which is designed to make pupils aware of some of the differences between life in Palestine 2000 years ago and life today – and also of some of the similarities. The game is played by up to four pupils, each of which is given a blank nine-squared lotto board of the type shown in Figure 5.1. A pack of 60 picture cards is prepared, consisting of 40 'correct' cards and 20 'wrong' cards. The former consist of a mixture of 20 'biblical times cards' that depict things that definitely relate to different aspects of life 2000 years ago (Roman soldiers, contemporary buildings, etc) and 20 'cross cards' that depict things that are common to biblical and modern times (farm animals, fish, bread, honey, etc). The latter depict things that definitely relate to modern life (a car, a telephone, a gas cooker, etc).

To play the game, the pack is shuffled and laid face down. The players then take turns to pick up the top card, decide whether it is a 'correct' card, ie either a 'biblical times card' or a 'cross card', and, if so, place it on one of the empty squares on their board. As each card is either accepted or rejected, the player involved should be encouraged to explain *why* it is being accepted or rejected, and the other players should be encouraged to say if they agree or disagree. The teacher should be brought in as an adjudicator if necessary. The game can either end when one player 'wins' by collecting nine 'correct cards', or can continue until all the players have done so. Such a game can again obviously be played at a number of different levels, with cards carrying both pictures and writing being used with older children, thus helping them to develop their reading skills. The 'correct-card/cross-card/wrong-card' approach could also be used in the study of *any* period of history by the 'patch method'. Teachers are again invited to devise their own games of this type.

Another game that could be used in the teaching of comparative religion is *Religions of the World*. This consists of a map of the world (with the outlines and names of individual countries shown) onto which pupils have to place coloured pieces representing the areas in which different major religions –

Christianity, Islam, Hinduism, Buddhism, etc – are practised. Such a game helps to show pupils that people living in different parts of the world have different religious beliefs, and also that many religions cover extremely wide areas. It also increases their knowledge of geography. Teachers are invited to try making up a game of this type for themselves, as simple or as complicated as they wish. The necessary information on the practice of different religions world-wide can be found in any large atlas.

Fostering creative and artistic expression

As with nursery children, games and simulations are again very useful in helping early-primary pupils develop their powers of creative and artistic expression. Role-playing simulations in which pupils act out situations drawn from everyday life or well-known historical or religious events are particularly useful for this purpose. Indeed, drama of all types – whether guided or free – is invariably an extremely powerful and effective way of reinforcing facts and ideas in young minds. Such drama is particularly effective if suitable 'props' can be made available, especially clothing appropriate to the scenario being acted out; young children *love* dressing up!

Suitably designed games and simulations can also be used to help children develop their oral and written story-telling skills. They might, for example, be asked to write a story based on a linear-jigsaw game, or produce their own drawing or painting of some episode from such a game that particularly appeals to them or excites their imagination. No doubt teachers can think of specific ways in which games and simulations can be used to help their own pupils develop their creative powers.

Detailed case study

Let us end this chapter by taking a detailed look at how games and simulations were built into a major curriculum-development project in one particular school – Towie Primary School in Aberdeenshire. This was another of the schools that took part in the 1990–91 Grampian Primary Industry Project, in which schools were invited to teach their pupils about the business side of industry through the medium of games and simulations and by forming links with local industrial firms.

Towie is a small school, and, at the time of the Project, had 25 pupils divided into two 'family-grouped' classes – a P1–4 class of 12 pupils and a P5–7 class of 13 pupils (such family grouping is typical of small rural Scottish schools). Both classes took part in the Project, both basing their work on the general theme of 'food'. The class teacher for the P1–4 group of pupils was Alison Robb, and it is her work on the Project that will be described in this case study.

Alison decided to build her Grampian Primary Industry Project round a well-known children's book – *Charlie and the Chocolate Factory* by Roald Dahl. This is about a young boy called Charlie, who lives with his parents and grandparents in a small house. Money is tight, and Charlie has few material possessions, but he is a kind, thoughtful boy who both loves and is loved by his family.

Mr Wonka is the owner of the chocolate factory which Charlie has to pass on his way to school every day. Charlie is fascinated by it, and dearly wishes he could see inside it. His grandfather is always telling him stories about Mr Wonka and his factory. One day, Mr Wonka announces that hidden in five of his chocolate bars, on sale throughout the world, are five 'golden tickets'. The lucky people who find these will be given a grand tour of his factory, and spend the whole day there.

Four rude, spoilt and obnoxious children – plus, of course, Charlie – each find a 'golden ticket', and the rest of the novel focuses on their tour of the factory. Mr Wonka tests the children as they walk around, and, one by one, they fail to meet his standards and are sent home – except for Charlie. He is eventually given the keys of the factory, and he and his family live there with Mr Wonka.

Alison chose this book because it is one that is loved by all children; the idea of winning a tour of a chocolate factory appeals instantly! On a more serious note, it allows children to see how five different characters react to their prize, and teaches pupils to think about others, be well mannered, and so on. It also formed an ideal basis for her project, which ran through the entire spring term of the 1990–91 session. Throughout this period, she read an average of two chapters of the book to her class every week. After reading each chapter, she discussed the plot, the behaviour of the different characters and other topics raised by the chapter with her pupils. Most of their classwork during the term was based on the book. This included:

- language work (writing summaries, comprehension work, discussions, etc)
- maths work (chocolate bar surveys, costs, money, change, etc)
- environmental studies (the story of chocolate, how the raw materials are grown, how it is produced, packaged and sold)
- expressive arts (art work, role-playing drama based on scenes from the book).

She also formed links with a nearby sweet factory (Deeside Candies of Ballater), taking her pupils on a tour of their factory and obtaining a wide range of background information from them. Because it would have been technically difficult for the children to make chocolate or sweets in the classroom, however, she based much of the practical side of the project on a related topic: 'making shortbread' (which the pupils could – and did – make themselves).

During the course of her project, Alison and her pupils developed two board games, both based on her secondary theme of 'making shortbread'. The first was the *Towie Shortbread Game*, a *Monopoly*-type board game involving collecting the ingredients for making shortbread, weighing them out, and then actually baking the shortbread in class. As they moved round the perimeter of the board, the pupils received step-by-step instructions on how to make shortbread by picking up inverted cards, arranged in the correct order, describing the various stages of the preparation and baking process.

This is a good example of how a simple game can be used both as a vehicle for reinforcing knowledge and understanding of a particular topic and as a vehicle for controlling and structuring a real-life activity. The game also helped to achieve a wide range of secondary educational objectives, including the development of psychomotor skills (those associated with weighing, measuring and other aspects of baking), helping the children to develop correct attitudes to hygiene, health and safety in the kitchen, helping them to develop their language skills (both written and oral), and their interpersonal and social skills. The game also encouraged the pupils to work together as a team, and gave them some idea of the amount of work and effort that has to go into producing simple things like shortbread. The only real weakness of the game was that most of the thinking was done *for* the pupils, in that the instruction cards were arranged in the correct order before the game started. It was found that the exercise proved too difficult for children of this age if the players had to sort out the order for themselves, although this would probably have worked with older children.

The second game developed for use in the project was *Shortbread Process* – another *Monopoly*-type game covering all stages of the commercial manufacture and marketing of shortbread. It was designed to follow on from the *Towie Shortbread Game* by giving the pupils an insight into the nature of the bakery business, particularly related to costs and profits. As they worked their way round the board, the children were given detailed basic information about the costs associated with the manufacture, packaging, distribution and sale of shortbread. At each stage, the pupils had to work out the overall costs using calculators, working in small cooperative groups in which the older children helped the younger ones. The object of the game was for each of the competing groups to work out a realistic selling price for their shortbread that would cover all their costs and make a reasonable profit.

As well as reinforcing the children's knowledge and understanding of the nature of the commercial bakery industry, *Shortbread Process* again helped the pupils to develop a wide range of useful process skills. These included language and counting skills, problem-solving skills, research skills, general group skills and interpersonal skills. It again also encouraged them to work together as a team. Both Alison and the authors were amazed at just how well the exercise worked, since conventional opinion had suggested that some of the sophisticated concepts that the game introduced would be beyond the capabilities of such young children to master. As it turned out, conventional opinion was wrong, and the children coped extremely well. Alison also felt that the game gave the pupils a genuine feel for the nature of business that could never have been achieved by more traditional teaching alone. By the end of the project, she was completely convinced of the power and effectiveness of games and simulations as teaching tools. Again, the authors hope that this description of her project will encourage other teachers working at the early-primary stage to try using similar exercises with their own pupils.

6

Using Games and Simulations with Upper-Primary and Lower-Secondary Pupils

This is the third of the four chapters that look in detail at how games and simulations can be used with pupils of different ages. It deals with their use at upper-primary/lower-secondary level, ie with pupils of age roughly 8–14 who are extending their general education prior to undertaking more specialized, subject-based education further up the secondary school.

Some basic features of upper-primary and lower-secondary education

This chapter deals with the later years of children's 'general' education, the period that builds upon the basic literacy and numeracy developed during the early-primary stages and prepares them for the more intensive, subject-based curriculum that they will follow in the latter stages of their secondary education. In some countries, eg the USA, the change from a general, broad-based curriculum to a specialized, subject-based curriculum is marked by a change of school – from 'elementary school' to 'high school' – at the age of roughly 14. In Britain, on the other hand, most children make the move from a 'primary school' to a 'secondary school' somewhat earlier – at the age of 11 or 12. When they do so, they start to be taught by subject-specialist teachers rather than by the generalist class teachers who were responsible for their primary education. Despite this change of school, however, the early stages of British secondary education are effectively an extension of the later stages of primary education, with children continuing to follow a common, fairly broad-based curriculum. Indeed, the Scottish curricular guidelines for the initial 'general' phase of statutory education cover the entire period from 5–14.

As with early-primary education, teachers working at upper-primary or lower-secondary level are invariably given a considerable amount of guidance regarding the *strategic direction* of the curriculum they are required to deliver, the *specific targets* they should be aiming to achieve at each stage, and the *teaching methods* they should employ in order to achieve these targets. Although such guidelines again vary from country to country and from one local education authority to another, they again all tend to include the following key elements. First, they all stress the importance of building on basic literacy by helping pupils to extend and develop their spoken-language, written-language and general communication skills. Second, they all stress the importance of building on basic numeracy by developing the children's computational, elementary mathematical and IT skills. In addition, they all help pupils to gain a better understanding of themselves and their environment, to become socially, morally and (in many countries) religiously aware, to develop important transferable skills such as problem-solving and decision-making, and to further develop their artistic and creative powers. In many cases, schools are again encouraged to build their teaching on a series of overall 'themes' that provide pupils with the opportunity to develop in the different areas listed.

How games and simulations can contribute to upper-primary and lower-secondary education

The authors have again found that classroom games and simulations are capable of making an important contribution to the teaching of all the key areas of the '8–14' curriculum. Such exercises can, however, be made considerably more demanding than those used at lower-primary level, and it can also be assumed that the great majority of the children will be literate and numerate, so the rules, resource materials and scenarios can be made correspondingly more sophisticated. Great care should still be taken to match the level of games and simulations to the state of development and ability of the children with whom they are to be used, however. This is particularly important if they are to be used with less-able children, or with children who are experiencing learning difficulties due to problems such as dyslexia. It is also still important that the exercises should relate to the children's own experience in so far as this is possible. Let us now see how games and simulations can be used to help develop the various types of knowledge and skills identified in the last section.

Developing language and communication skills

As shown in earlier chapters, games and simulations are ideal for helping children to develop their language and communication skills. Any exercises that involve competitive play or working in groups, for example, automatically provide situations in which they can practise and extend their spoken-language and oral-communication skills, often in highly motivating and enjoyable situations. Games and simulations can also be used to help them develop their reading and interpretative skills, and, in situations where they have to produce written or word-processed materials, their written-language skills as well. All types of games and simulations can be used for this purpose – card games, board games, simple manual exercises and computer-based exercises.

Exercises of the latter type are particularly useful for helping individual pupils to develop the basic skills associated with the use of language. Figure 5.3 showed a commercial package of this type designed for use with younger pupils, aged 5–8. Figure 6.1 shows a package from the same company designed for use further up the primary school, with pupils aged 8–11. This is again carefully designed to fit in with the appropriate stages of the English National Curriculum. Teachers might find it useful to carry out a detailed comparison of the games included in the two packages, looking at the specific activities they involve, the particular skills they are designed to develop, and the demands they make of the pupils. They constitute a good example of a stepped series of games designed to help children develop their language skills in a systematic, progressive way. Many packages of this general type are now available commercially, and teachers should again study the latest catalogues to see which would be most suitable for their own classes. Again, make sure that any chosen packages will work on the machines that are available to your pupils.

Two of the projects that were carried out by schools taking part in the 1990–91 Grampian Primary Industry Project showed just how useful games and simulations can be in helping upper-primary pupils develop their language skills. The class teachers involved – Elizabeth Macleod of Westhill Primary School and Hilda Creighton of Dales Park Primary School, Peterhead – were both responsible for teaching P7 classes containing 28 pupils at the time, and both decided to base their projects on the setting up of a simulated newspaper company and the production and selling of its newspaper.

Figure 6.2 shows three of the Westhill 'reporters' carrying out an interview for their newspaper during one of the sponsors' visits to their school, while Figure 6.3 shows two of the 'copywriters' preparing final copy. The school was fortunate to possess a fairly sophisticated computer facility at the time – eight networked 'Nimbus' workstations together with peripheral equipment such as a scanner and a high-quality printer – and this made the task of actually producing the newspaper very much easier. By the end of the project,

BBC/MASTER/COMPACT
*ARCHIMEDES   ELECTRON

READING PACK 4: Age 8-11
Cassette:£9.95   Disc:£12.95

* *Archimedes version only available as part of "Bumper Pack 1"*
(see end of catalogue)

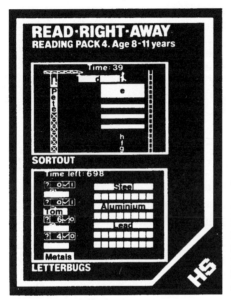

Game 1:"Sortout"
(Alphabetical sorting of letters/words)
A crane and 2 eager workmen are on hand to help each player sort a random pile of letters/words into alphabetical order, constructing a building with the letters/words in the process. Each player's score and time is attractively displayed at the end of the game, with winner(s) highlighted.

Game 2:"Letterbugs"
(Unscrambling hidden words.)
Players have a series of 8 words (from 1 of 15 categories), that are hidden somewhere behind lines of coloured squares. Each player has a "Letterbug" which they use to uncover the words, either by "looking" (only a limited number of "looks" are allowed to each player), or by guessing the hidden letter from the other letters uncovered and the clue at the bottom of the screen.

"..I suspect these are the sort of programs children will enjoy taking home in days to come, for learning with these really is fun, and mums and dads will play with them after children are tucked up in bed just for the pleasure of the graphics."
- A & B COMPUTING

NATIONAL CURRICULUM KEY STAGE 2
ATTAINMENT TARGETS: ENGLISH 2,4

Figure 6.1 The publicity material on two computer games designed to help older primary pupils develop their language skills.

Figure 6.2 Three of the Westhill Primary School 'reporters' interviewing the Managing Director of the main sponsoring company, Goodfellow Associates, Ltd, for the class newspaper that they produced during the Grampian Primary Industry Project.

Figure 6.3 Two of the Westhill 'copywriters' using one of the school's eight networked Nimbus workstations to prepare final copy for their class newspaper.

the pupils were completely 'at home' with the associated technology. Dales Park did not have anything like such sophisticated equipment at its disposal (simply three 'Videowriters' plus a basic printer), but still managed to produce six issues of its newspaper over the 12 weeks of the project.

Extended whole-class simulations of the type carried out at Westhill and Dales Park are ideal for helping pupils to develop all aspects of their language and communication skills, together with a wide range of other skills, eg IT skills, planning, decision-making and problem-solving skills, artistic and design skills, and interpersonal skills. They also give the children first-hand experience of running a business, of working as part of a team, and of playing specific roles within such a team (in the two projects described, these included the editor, deputy editor, artistic director, advertising manager, sales manager, reporters, copywriters, and so on). Both the teachers involved became totally convinced of the power and effectiveness of such large-scale role-playing simulations as educational tools.

At Dales Park, the children's knowledge and experience of the newspaper industry were further enhanced by the development of two board games for use in conjunction with the main role-playing simulation. The first was *Scoop* – a *Monopoly*-type game in which players took the role of freelance reporters trying to scoop stories. By landing on particular squares, players won the option of scooping specific stories, and had to decide whether to take them on by weighing potential income against associated expenses. The winner was the player making most money after a set playing time. The second was *A Reporter's Year*, a snakes and ladders-type game simulating the ups and downs of the life of a reporter (scooping stories, winning promotion, losing stories to a rival newspaper, missing deadlines, etc). Both games helped to extend the pupils' knowledge and understanding of newspaper terminology, and also helped them to appreciate the risky nature of the life of a reporter, particularly one working on a 'freelance' basis. They proved to be an ideal complement to the main simulation.

Developing computational, mathematical and IT skills

As we saw in Chapters 4 and 5, games and simulations can prove extremely useful in helping children to develop pre-maths skills and basic numerical skills. With older children, they can be used to build upon this foundational work by helping them to develop more advanced computational skills, to prepare them for the study of true mathematics higher up the school, and by further developing their IT skills. As with the development of language and communication skills, all forms of games and simulations can be used for this purpose, with computer-based exercises being particularly effective because of their suitability for developing numerical and mathematical skills of all types.

Computer-based games and simulations are especially useful in helping individual pupils extend and develop their computational skills. Figure 5.5 showed a suite of such exercises designed to help younger pupils (aged 5–7) develop basic number skills. Figure 6.4 shows materials produced by the same company for use with slightly older pupils, aged 7–12. These are again designed to fit in with the appropriate stages of the English National Curriculum, helping children to master the basic arithmetical processes of addition, subtraction, multiplication and division. Teachers might again find it useful to carry out a detailed comparison of the exercises included in the two packages in terms of the activities that they involve, the skills they are designed to develop and the demands that they make of the pupils. The suites shown in Figures 5.5 and 6.4 again constitute a good example of a stepped series of games, designed to help children to develop their basic arithmetical skills in a systematic, progressive manner. Many such packages are now available to teachers, who are advised to study the latest educational catalogues to see what would best suit their particular needs.

Games that ask pupils to apply their arithmetical skills by carrying out calculations based on the processes involved are also extremely useful in helping them to become more confident and proficient in using these skills. A good example of a game of this type is the *Culraggie Whisky Game* shown in Figure 6.5. This was developed by Howard Edge of Tomintoul Primary School, who ran a project on the whisky industry with his P6/7 class as part of the 1990–91 Grampian Primary Industry Project. The game is based on the various stages in the commercial manufacture of whisky, which is carried out in several places in the Tomintoul area. (It is rumoured that the *private* manufacture of the same product also thrives in the Tomintoul area – provided that those involved can continue to escape the attention of the local excisemen!)

As can be seen from Figure 6.5, the *Culraggie Whisky Game* is a *Monopoly*-type board game. Players start with a credit balance of £200,000, and have to progress round the board from the START to the FINISH square by throwing a single die, the object being to make as large an operating profit as possible as they do so. Landing on certain squares causes players to gain or lose money, as does landing on the 'whisky card' and 'production card' squares. A typical 'good' card might tell the player that 'Japanese sales have risen; credit your account by £20,000', while a typical 'bad' card might inform them that 'You are fined £10,000 for polluting the river; debit your account'. As they move round the board, players have to maintain credit or debit accounts by taking note of all the financial transactions that the game involves. The final credit or debit balances are calculated once the game is over, the winner being the player who has made the biggest profit.

CARRYADD: Age 7-11
Cassette:£6.95   Disc:£9 .95

BBC/MASTER/COMPACT
ARCHIMEDES

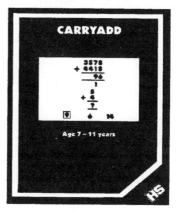

The two programs in "Carryadd" really help children to get to grips with the processes of addition and subtraction, starting at the earliest stages and progressing through to addition and subtraction of 5 digits with "carrying".
Each step is shown clearly on screen, and faithfully reproduces the way in which a child would actually write down the sum.
"Press any key" facility means that young or physically handicapped children find the programs easy to use.

NATIONAL CURRICULUM KEY STAGES 1 & 2
ATTAINMENT TARGET: MATHS 2

BBC/MASTER/COMPACT
ARCHIMEDES ELECTRON

BERT BOOT: Age 8-12
Cassette:£6.95 Disc:£7.95

Even working out multiplication and division problems can be fun, when you have "Bert Boot", the intrepid insect squasher, to help you!
This entertaining game takes children through the process of solving multiplication and division problems in 8 carefully graded stages. When an answer has been entered, Bert performs his relentless task and gives a visual representation of the problem and the right answer. If 80% or more your answers are correct, you can play "Beat the Boots", an exciting arcade game in which your insects have to tackle droves of vicious footwear reach the safety of the jampots!"

"It is certainly the most amazing visual representation I have seen yet in a piece of educational software"
- EDUCATIONAL COMPUTING

NATIONAL CURRICULUM KEY STAGES 1,2 & 3
ATTAINMENT TARGETS: MATHS 2

Figure 6.4 The publicity material on two suites of computer exercises designed to help older primary pupils develop basic arithmetical skills.

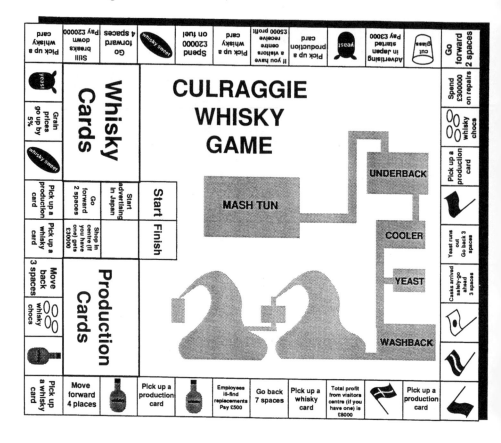

Figure 6.5 The board used in the *Culraggie Whisky Game*.

Developing knowledge of themselves and their environment

Games and simulations are also extremely effective vehicles for teaching pupils about themselves and about their environment. Two of the board games that will be described in Chapter 9 are good examples of exercises of the former type. The first, *Health Snakes and Ladders*, is designed to reinforce class teaching that certain things are good for your health and that others are harmful. The second, *Microbe Attack* is designed to reinforce pupils' knowledge and understanding of the way in which invading microbes have to be destroyed by the body's immune system in order to prevent them from causing disease. Both games were developed during the 1980s for use in teaching the 'Healthy Bodies' section of the Scottish Foundation and General Level Science Curriculum, and can be used at both upper-primary and lower-secondary levels. They show how simple classroom games can be used to support basic teaching by reinforcing the key facts and principles covered in a context that the children find stimulating and enjoyable.

Another simple classroom game of this general type is *Survival*, a game that was developed for use in teaching the 'Environment' section of the Scottish Foundation and General Level Science Curriculum. It can again be used at both upper-primary and lower-secondary levels. The game is designed for use as a follow-up to a lesson (or series of lessons) on the competition for food and living space and the predator–prey relationship.

Survival is based on an imaginary island (see Figure 6.6) whose main inhabitants are two species of predators called snappers and gobblers, which eat kidlings. The island can only support a total of six breeding pairs of predators, each of which occupies a definite territory (the six areas shown on the map). On average, one territory becomes vacant every year due to the death of one (or both) of the members of the breeding pair of predators that occupy it. When this happens, the territory is taken over by a new breeding pair, either of the same species or of the rival species. Each round of the game thus represents one year, and consists of a throw of a single standard die (to determine which territory becomes vacant) and a single tossing of a coin (to determine which species takes it over). At the start of the game, the north of the island (territories 1, 2 and 3) is occupied by snappers, and the south (territories 4, 5 and 6) by gobblers. Each round involves first removing the token representing one of the species from the map (as a result of the throw of the die) and then replacing it by a token of the same or different type (as a result of the toss of the coin). The game ends when one species becomes extinct, or at the end of an agreed period, when the winning species is the one that occupies most territory.

Survival can be used in a number of different ways, eg:

Kidling Island

Figure 6.6 Kidling Island – the 'board' on which *Survival* is played.

- as a full-class exercise, in the form of a competition between two halves of the class, with the 'board' being displayed using the OHP
- as a full-class exercise in which the pupils play the game in pairs, each with their own board and other materials
- as a 'pacing exercise' carried out by pairs of pupils
- as a 'fun' game (serving a reinforcement function) played outwith class time.

The game can also be used as the basis of a case study in statistical fluctuation.

A second game that was developed for use in teaching the 'Environment' section of the Scottish Foundation and General Level Science Curriculum is *Lebensraum*, which will also be described in Chapter 9. This is based on the competition between rival species as they spread into new territory. It can again be used at both upper-primary and lower-secondary levels.

Contributing to their social, moral and religious education

Another general area in which games and simulations are particularly effective is in helping children to develop all the various interpersonal and social skills that are so important for success in later life and in contributing to their moral and religious education. A number of exercises that can be used for such purposes with younger children have been described in Chapters 4 and 5. With older children, the exercises can be made progressively more demanding and sophisticated, introducing them to new concepts and ideas appropriate to their level of development and educational needs. Simulation exercises that involve children in *role-play* of various sorts are particularly effective in achieving interpersonal and affective objectives of the type that are so important in social, moral and religious education. The lessons learned during such exercises tend to last, since the experiences become deeply embedded in the minds of the children.

A good example of an exercise of this general type is *Barter*, a whole-class simulation/game developed by J. Mortimer during the 1980s for use with children aged 10–13 in a patch study of the Middle Ages. The game was designed to help them to understand what it must have been like to live in a highly stratified society where barter at the local market was the main mechanism whereby goods were exchanged. It requires a minimum of 28 participants, each of whom is given a card describing the role that they will play – peasant, craftsman or merchant. The information on the back of the card indicates the goods the player has to sell, the items they have to acquire, and the items that they should not be prepared to accept. The class teacher plays the role of Lord of the Manor, with complete authority over the market and what goes on in it. To prepare for the game, younger pupils make cardboard cutouts representing the various goods that will be used (vegetables, poultry, farm animals, other foods, clothing, artefacts of various types, and so on), together with cardboard baskets in which to hold these. With older pupils, a 'score card' method of recording transactions can be used. The game is normally played over a set period, during which the players try to achieve their individual trading objectives. It is followed by a detailed debriefing, during which the lessons learned from the game are discussed, analysed and related to modern life.

Role-playing simulations can also be used in moral and religious education. Children can, for example, be asked to act out important episodes from the lives of great religious leaders and prophets, either formally (using a prepared script) or informally (with the children 'ad-libbing' their own dialogue). A useful variation of such role-play is to get the children to act out parables and similar stories with a moral message in a modern setting. This is an extremely powerful device to help them relate the underlying message to their own lives. An example might be the acting out of the parable of the Good Samaritan, in which the victim is left beaten up by muggers and is rescued and looked after by a passing group of children. Such simulations can be followed up by detailed class discussions, after which the children can be asked to write essays on what they have learned.

Computer simulations and databases can also be used extremely effectively in social, moral and religious education. One such package (*Damascus Reporter,* by Geoffrey Bagnall) places the user in the role of a 'reporter' for a 'newspaper' just at the time when the early Christians were making their presence known in Damascus. A young Pharisee, Saul of Tarsus, is organizing a vicious persecution of them – or is he? It is up to the 'reporter' to find out by exploring the material made available through the package. Such simulations are usually more suitable for individual use rather than for class use, although they can form the basis of a whole-class discussion once everyone has had the chance to use them.

Developing high-level process skills

As we saw in Chapter 2, games and simulations are particularly effective vehicles for helping children to develop high-level transferable process skills such as problem-solving and decision-making. A good example of an exercise that can be used for this purpose at upper-primary and lower-secondary levels is *Which Material?*, which was developed for use in the teaching of the 'Materials' section of the Scottish Foundation and General Level Science Curriculum. It is intended to be used as a follow-up to (or as an integral part of) a taught lesson or series of lessons on the use of materials. It is designed to make the pupils aware of the many factors that have to be taken into consideration when choosing the material from which a particular item is to be made (the frame for a chair that is to be put to heavy use, the casing of an electric plug, a general-purpose kitchen spoon, the hull of a lifeboat, and so on). To run the exercise, the class is divided into small groups of 4–6 pupils, each of which is assigned a different item and is asked to do the following:

- try to think of 3 or 4 different materials that could be used to manufacture the item
- list all the advantages and disadvantages of each material that they can think of
- decide which they consider would be the best material, taking account of all relevant factors.

Each pupil is given a copy of the worksheet shown in Figure 6.7 on which to carry out their work. The exercise is rounded off by holding a plenary debriefing session, in which the various groups report back to the rest of the class on how they reached their decisions, and these decisions are discussed and criticized.

The *North Sea Auction* simulation/game that was described in Chapter 3 is another good example of an exercise that can be used to help pupils develop problem-solving and decision-making skills. The 'older' version of the

WHICH MATERIAL?

PUPIL WORKSHEET

Item to be manufactured:

Possible material	Advantages	Disadvantages

Recommended material:

Figure 6.7 The pupil worksheet used in *Which Material?*

exercise, in which teams of pupils have to agree on their overall bidding strategy for the auction and submit a detailed set of bids based on this, is particularly useful in this regard.

Fostering creative and artistic expression

As with younger pupils, games and simulations can also be used to help upper-primary and lower-secondary pupils develop their powers of creative and artistic expression. Role-playing simulations in which the pupils act out episodes from history, religious teaching or everyday life are again particularly useful for this purpose. Such role-playing exercises can also be used as the basis of creative-writing exercises, artistic work such as painting or model-making, and so on. The Westhill and Dales Park 'class newspaper' projects that were described earlier in this chapter are particularly good examples of how whole-class simulations can be used to help pupils develop a wide range of creative and artistic skills. The specific skills developed by these projects included creative writing, graphic design, and general artistic skills.

Detailed Case Study

Let us end this chapter by taking a detailed look at how games and simulations were built into a major curriculum-development project in one particular school – Anderson's Primary School, Forres. This was yet another of the schools that participated in the 1990–91 Grampian Primary Industry Project. The class teacher involved was one of the authors – Joannie Fowlie – who ran a project based on the engineering industry with her P7 class of 33 pupils. This is the project that will now be described.

The main object of the Grampian Primary Industry Project was to help the participating pupils to learn about the business side of industry through the use of classroom games and simulations and the formation of school–industry links. Joannie Fowlie decided to base her project on the heavy-engineering industry, since her school was fairly close to William Reid Engineering of Forres, and they were willing to act as her local link company.

After Joannie had made several visits to the firm herself, Mr Rod Bush, William Reid's Building Projects Supervisor, paid a visit to her class. He presented an entertaining and informative picture of the work carried out by the firm, describing how they were currently working on a major contract that involved supplying the steel structure for a new building at Shetland Fisheries College, in Scalloway. He explained how they had won the contract, and described all the various stages that had to be gone through in order to fulfil it. When he told the children that 250 tons of steel were required at an approximate price of £350 per ton, nearly all of the pupils – even the least enthusiastic maths pupils – had their pencils out trying to calculate the total cost. Mr Bush's visit gave rise to a stimulating class discussion, and got the project off to an excellent start.

The children then paid a visit to the premises of William Reid Engineering, where they were given a conducted tour of the entire works, in three groups. Even those with behavioural problems were totally engrossed and, on return to school, the pupils discussed what they had seen and heard and generally shared information. Some had scavenged and picked up various bits of rejected steel strips, nuts and bolts, etc. This, in turn, led to what might be done with them.

Welding was discussed, and this led to the discussion of other aspects of the engineering industry, such as the need for safety.

Soon afterwards, a senior member of William Reid's staff visited the school and spoke to the class about how a job is costed, giving detailed information about the economic aspects of the Shetland Fisheries College contract. A local bank manager also visited the school, describing how banks become involved in projects of this type, and explaining the processes whereby loans are taken out, borrowed capital is repaid, interest is paid, and so on. Groups of children then made further visits to William Reid Engineering to discuss further aspects of the business side of the engineering industry.

It had already been decided that the school's Grampian Primary Industry Project would be built round a whole-class role-playing simulation exercise in which the class would be divided into six competing teams, each representing a different engineering company trying to win the contract for a particular job. It was originally intended that the problem to be tackled would be that of designing and building a new entrance to Forres Public Library from the car park. This proved a little too demanding for the pupils, however, so it was decided to change the problem to something simpler – tendering for a contract to manufacture and deliver a single steel beam to Shetland Fisheries College, to the specification incorporated in the William Reid contract. The details of this new problem were discussed with staff of William Reid, and the six competing 'companies' soon started work on their tenders.

The six teams had to carry out all the same processes that a real engineering firm would have to go through when preparing an actual competitive tender. First, they had to carry out all the necessary background research, finding out about all the technical, financial and other factors involved in the work. Then they had to cost the purchase of the steel from which the beam would be made, and choose a suitable supplier. Then, they had to manufacture the beam, and arrange for it to be galvanized and painted. Finally, they had to make arrangements to deliver it to Shetland Fisheries College, by road and sea. The teams worked in great secrecy, in order to prevent their rivals from finding out about the details of their tenders. The exercise reached its climax with the presentation of the final tenders to William Reid, who decided which was the most realistic and competitive and chose the winner on this basis.

The revised version of the competitive-tender simulation turned out to be a great success. Not only did it reinforce what the children had learned about the engineering industry from William Reid; it also provided a stimulus for the pupils to *find out more for themselves*, thus helping them to develop basic information-gathering and research skills. It also gave them the sort of first-hand insight into the operation of an engineering company that they could never have received simply by being told about what goes on in such an organization. Finally, it helped them to develop a whole range of useful skills, including team skills, interpersonal skills, communication skills, IT skills, problem-solving skills, decision-making skills and planning skills. From the experience gained through the Grampian Primary Industry Project and similar initiatives, the authors have concluded that extended whole-class simulations of this type are one of the most powerful and effective tools at the disposal of the modern teacher. They work!

As well as running the major simulation described above, Joannie Fowlie and her pupils developed a number of board games in connection with their class project. The most successful of these was *Contract 3-5*, a *Monopoly*-type game that made use of a triangular board rather than the conventional square board (see Figure 6.8). The object of the game was to acquire three 'contract cards' (or five, if a longer game was wanted), and to obtain the raw materials needed to fulfil the contracts. The triangular 'squares' round the perimeter of the board were colour-coded, corresponding to the five sets of cards placed in the interior. On landing on a square of a particular colour, the appropriate card was collected. The 'Hazard' cards (corresponding to 'Chance' cards in *Monopoly*) introduced an element of the unexpected. Another interesting feature of the game was that the set of simulated money

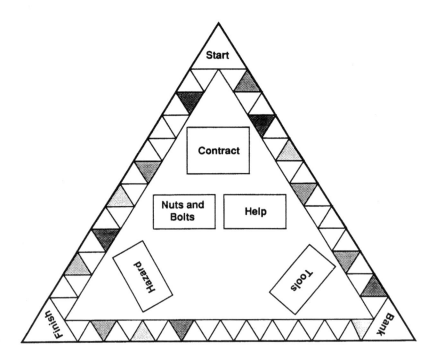

Figure 6.8 The triangular board used in *Contract 3-5*.

was produced by photocopying actual banknotes, something that required the permission of the local bank. The bank also lent them specimens of the necessary banknotes, some of which were of high denomination.

Contract 3-5 turned out to be an extremely useful complement to the main role-playing simulation. It helped to reinforce the pupils' knowledge and understanding of what is involved in obtaining and fulfilling engineering contracts, and did so in a context that the children found both enjoyable and stimulating. It also helped them to develop a number of useful skills, including number and language skills, general interpersonal and communication skills, basic accounting skills, and decision-making skills. The game also helped to make them appreciate the competitive and risky nature of business. The children also got a great deal out of designing the game and making up playing sets, a topic that will be dealt with in more detail in Chapter 10.

7

Using Games and Simulations with Older Secondary Pupils

This is the last of the four chapters that look in detail at how games and simulations can be used with pupils of different ages. It deals with their use with older secondary pupils of age roughly 14–18.

Some basic features of later-secondary education

As we saw in the last chapter, the statutory education that children undergo in most Western countries generally changes significantly in character at the age of about 14. Below that age, children receive a general, broad-based education, and do not normally have the opportunity to specialize in particular subjects. At about 14, however, their education begins to become progressively more specialized, and they have to start to choose which particular subjects they wish to study further. As they progress through the later stages of their secondary education, they generally concentrate on fewer and fewer subjects, finishing up studying five or six at most. In England, which has the most specialized secondary-education system of all, they generally study only three subjects during their final years at secondary school.

Secondary education also differs from primary education in that the teaching is carried out by subject specialists rather than by generalists. The curriculum is also much more tightly specified, with most teachers having to follow a standard syllabus designed to prepare pupils to sit externally-set examinations. There is thus much less scope for curricular variation and experiment at secondary level, since pupils have only a limited time to study each of their specialist subjects, and teachers tend to concentrate on what *has* to be covered to enable them to pass their exams. Secondary teaching thus tends to be highly content-centred, although there is an increasing realization that it is also important to help pupils to develop the various *process* skills that are so important for success in later life. Indeed, if we accept the definition of true education as 'what is left after the facts have been forgotten', the development of such process skills assumes even greater importance. These are certainly the skills that employers are increasingly expecting the products of our schools and colleges to possess.

How games and simulations can contribute to later-secondary education

If time can be found to fit them into the curriculum, classroom games and simulations are capable of making just as valuable a contribution to later-secondary education as to the earlier stages discussed in Chapters 4–6. Furthermore, they are capable of contributing to both the content and the process aspects of such education, as we will now demonstrate by looking at some of the main ways in which they can be used with later-secondary classes. When used at this level, the exercises can, of course, be much more demanding and sophisticated than those used at lower levels, although it is still important to ensure that they are properly matched to the capabilities of the participating pupils.

Reinforcing the teaching of basic facts and principles

Games and simulations are no more effective than more conventional teaching methods such as face-to-face teaching and individualized study in teaching the basic facts and principles of a subject. They are, however, particularly effective in *reinforcing* and *supporting* the teaching of such basic facts and principles, eg by providing practice in their use, demonstrating applications, and providing illustrative case studies.

Two of the card games that are described in Chapter 9 provide excellent examples of the way in which classroom games can be used in such a supportive role. The first, *Formulon,* (see Figure 9.5) is designed to reinforce the teaching of the way different types of elements and ions combine to form chemical compounds, with players having to use their cards to build up legitimate compounds. The second, *Chemsyn,* (see Figure 9.6) is designed to reinforce the teaching of basic organic chemistry, with players having to produce sequences and patterns that show how different organic compounds can be transformed one into another. Both are good examples of exercises where the 'educational' and 'gaming' elements are well integrated, since pupils cannot play them successfully without understanding the underlying chemistry.

Another good example of a package that was designed specifically to support the teaching of basic facts and principles is *Licensed to Drill.* This was developed by Phillips Petroleum during the mid-1980s as an aid to the teaching of economics at upper-secondary and lower-tertiary levels. The package consists of a video based on the development of their 'Maureen' field in the North Sea, a 24-page booklet on the field, and a 120-page Teacher's Guide dealing with the economics of offshore oil development. The latter, which was written for Phillips by Henry Ellington and Eric Addinall, incorporates a whole range of games, simulations and case studies on seven aspects of the development process, some manual and some computer-based. Most of these exercises are designed to demonstrate the application of specific economic principles or procedures. The exercises that are incorporated in the different chapters of the Teacher's Guide are listed and outlined below.

Chapter 1 A background discussion on the North Sea petroleum industry

Class activity 1(a)
A manual case study on the history of the North Sea petroleum industry in which the students plot the positions of fields on a map of the area.

Class activity 1(b)
An individual or group project on the local, regional or national impact of the North Sea petroleum industry followed by a class discussion.

Chapter 2 The search for offshore oil and gas

Class activity 2(a)
A role-playing simulation/game in which teams of pupils representing oil companies take part in an auction for 30 newly available concessions that show varying degrees of promise. (The complete package for this exercise is given at the end of Chapter 3, under the name of *North Sea Auction.*)

Class activity 2(b)
A manual case study that involves determining the cost of drilling an exploration or appraisal well in the North Sea.

Class activity 2(c)
A manual case study that introduces the six simulated fields on which many of the subsequent class activities are built. (These fields – *Uniform*, *Victor*, *Whisky*, *X-ray*, *Yankee* and *Zulu* – are all modelled on actual North Sea fields, and cover the full range of types and sizes that operating companies have to deal with – see Figure 7.1.)

Comparative data on Uniform, Victor, Whisky, X-ray, Yankee and Zulu fields

Name of Field	Uniform	Victor	Whisky	X-ray	Yankee	Zulu
Location	E. of Edinburgh	W. of Shetlands	E. of Wick	E. of Aberdeen	N.E. of Shetlands	E. of Shetlands
Weather conditions	Good	Very poor	Moderate	Moderate	Poor	Poor
Water depth over field (m)	75	120	90	60	180	120
Depth of reservoir below seabed (m)	1,820	1,440	1,950	3,850	1,000	1,600
Geological condition of reservoir	Good	Faulted	Good	Good	Faulted	Badly Faulted
Total recoverable oil reserves (million barrels)	100	1,500	500	1,200	600	150
Total recoverable gas reserves (billion cubic feet)	None – gas to be re-injected	1,000	None – gas to be re-injected	None – gas to be re-injected	150	None – gas to be re-injected
Producing life of field (years)	13	24	22	24	21	13
Method of landing oil	Shuttle tankers	2 pipelines (1 oil; 1 gas)	Pipeline	Pipeline	2 pipelines (1 oil; 1 gas)	Shuttle tankers
Capital cost of developing field at 1985 prices (£ million)	462	3,850	1,350	2,860	1,995	910
Escalated capital cost of developing field (£ million)	569	4,745	1,667	3,606	2,416	1,056
Total revenue from field in escalated terms (£ million)	3,793	85,917	25,412	60,332	30,979	5,728
Total operating costs (escalated) (£ million)	1,024	25,173	6,862	19,079	9,421	1,993
Total government take (escalated) (£ million)	942	47,278	12,576	31,737	13,924	1,384
Total profit from field (escalated) (£ million)	1,258	8,721	4,309	5,909	5,219	1,295
Payout (years)	5·7	6·1	5·9	6·3	6·9	6·4
NTIR	3·21	2·84	3·59	2·64	3·16	2·23
NPV (at 25% discount rate) (£ million)	108	192	136	351	–48	–67
IRR (%)	39·0%	27·6%	30·1%	32·9%	23·9%	21·2%
Ranking as an investment prospect (1-6)						
Overall assessment as an investment prospect (good, marginal or bad)						

Figure 7.1 The student worksheet used in Class Activity 4(e) in the *Licensed to Drill* suite of games, simulations and case studies.

Chapter 3 Estimating the cost of a possible field development

Class activity 3(a)
A simulated case study that involves comparing the relative economic merits of different platform deployment strategies for developing a large offshore field.

Class activity 3(b)
A simulated case study that involves comparing the economics of pipelines and shuttle tankers for landing oil from different sizes of field at different distances from a suitable landfall.

Class activity 3(c)
A manual case study that involves determining the overall capital costs of developing the six simulated fields introduced in Class Activity 2(c).

Class activity 3(d)
A manual case study that involves determining the escalated investment profiles for the development of the six simulated fields.

Chapter 4 The development decision

Class activity 4(a)
A computer-based case study involving generating detailed cash-flow profiles for the six simulated fields, and hence determining their 'payback times' by plotting their 'J-curves'.

Class activity 4(b)
A manual case study involving using these profiles to calculate the 'NTIR' (number of times investment is returned) for each of the six simulated fields.

Class activity 4(c)
A manual case study involving using the cash-flow profiles to calculate the 'net present value' (NPV) of each of the six fields.

Class activity 4(d)
A computer-based case study involving the calculation of the 'IRR' (internal rate of return on capital invested) for each of the six fields.

Class activity 4(e)
A manual case study involving the overall evaluation and comparison of the

six fields as investment prospects. (The worksheet supplied to pupils for this exercise is shown in Figure 7.1. Teachers might like to try the exercise themselves. The model solution is given in Table 7.1 on p.109.)

Chapter 5 The financial management of a project

Class activity 5(a)
A manual case study involving investigating different possible methods of raising the capital for a major project.

Class activity 5(b)
A computer-based case study involving investigating the effect on profitability of investing in 'enhanced recovery' (use of artificial methods to increase the amount of oil that can be uplifted from a field).

Chapter 6 Murphy's Law

Class activity 6(a)
A computer-based case study that involves finding how a field's profitability is likely to be affected by changes (up or down) in its recoverable reserves due to unforeseen factors.

Class activity 6(b)
A computer-based case study that involves finding how a field's profitability is likely to be affected by changes in the price of oil.

Class activity 6(c)
A computer-based case study that involves finding how a field's profitability is likely to be affected by changes in fiscal policy.

Chapter 7 What happens to the revenue?

Class activity 7(a)
A manual case study on the likely uses of the revenue from the six hypothetical fields.

Class activity 7(b)
A manual case study on the social and economic benefits to the UK from North Sea oil and gas.

Class activity 7(c)
A manual case study on how oil companies use their profits.

The various exercises included in the *Licensed to Drill* package enable a group of pupils or students to apply basic economic and accounting principles to virtually all aspects of the development of an offshore oilfield, thus providing a realistic and interesting context for the demonstration of the application of the theoretical parts of their course. The package is also a good example of the way in which a linked series of exercises can be built round a single theme. It also shows how computer-based and manual exercises can be used to complement and support one another.

Developing higher-cognitive skills

We have seen that games, simulations and case studies are extremely effective in helping to develop *higher-cognitive skills* of all types. They are particularly effective in developing multi-faceted skills relating to such things as problem-solving, decision-making and creative thinking, and, in such areas, probably constitute one of the most powerful weapons in our educational armoury. This has long been recognized by business schools in all parts of the world, most of which rely heavily on the 'case-study method' that was originally developed at Harvard Business School during the 1950s. This involves exposing students to a carefully planned series of case studies – some simulated, some based on real life – through which they develop and hone all the various higher-level skills that are needed to succeed in business. Such exercises can range from fairly straightforward exercises of the simple manual type to highly sophisticated computer simulations and simulation/games. These techniques are now also widely used in teaching subjects such as economics, business management and accountancy at secondary-school level.

Many of the exercises included in the *Licensed to Drill* package described in the previous section include the development of higher-cognitive skills among their objectives. The 'older' version of *North Sea Auction* described at the end of Chapter 3, for example, is specifically designed to help the participants develop their problem-solving and decision-making skills. So is the exercise on the evaluation of the six simulated fields as investment prospects that is shown in Figure 7.1. Although this is based on 1985 prices, it is still a highly realistic exercise on investment appraisal that requires a high level of data processing, evaluative and decision-making skill on the part of the participants. If you have not already done so, try it for yourself, and see if you rank and rate the six fields in the same way as the authors of the exercise (see model solution in Table 7.1 on p.109 at end of chapter).

Another exercise that can be used to help pupils in the later years of secondary schools to develop their problem-solving, decision-making and planning skills is *Power for Pemang*. The original version of this exercise was published by the Schools Liaison Service of the Institution of Electrical Engineers in 1979 under the name of *Power for Elaskay*. A simplified version (the *Alternative Energy Project*) was subsequently published by the Association for Science Education in 1981, for use in the teaching of their highly innovative 'Science in Society' course. Both exercises involved drawing up a 50-year rolling programme for meeting the future electricity requirements of a hypothetical Scottish offshore island (Elaskay) by exploiting the island's natural energy resources – peat, solar energy, wind energy, tidal energy and hydroelectric power. An updated version of the exercise based on an East Asian scenario was developed by Henry Ellington in 1989, and was subsequently published by the IEE's Schools Liaison Service. This has the same basic scenario as the original exercises, except that the island on which it is based (Pemang) is located in the East Indies rather than off the west coast of Scotland, and one of the possible sources of energy (Elaskay's peat bog) has been replaced by a tropical rain forest. The island on which the scenario of *Power for Pemang* is based is shown in Figure 7.2.

For the first stage of *Power for Pemang*, the class is divided into five small groups, each of which carries out a detailed case study on the technical feasibility and economic viability of exploiting one of the five possible sources of energy that are available on the island. They do this by using the information provided in their group-instruction sheets to complete worksheets of the type shown in Figure 7.3 (the worksheet used by the group studying hydroelectric power). Once they have completed their case studies, the groups report on their findings to the rest of the class, and the pupils complete the station data proforma shown in Figure 7.4; this shows the completed version of the proforma, containing detailed technical and economic data on all the possible schemes for generating electricity on the island.

For the second stage of the exercise, the class is divided into two large competing teams, each of which has to draw up a 50-year rolling programme to satisfy Pemang's future electricity requirements by meeting the demand curve shown in Figure 7.5. (Readers might like to try the exercise for themselves, and should note that the island's existing electricity generation plant will all have to be shut down in five years' time at the latest, due to 'old age'.) The two teams then present their proposed schemes, and the teacher decides which is the most promising. The exercise ends with a debriefing session in which the work of the exercise is reviewed, and any issues raised by the participants discussed.

Power for Elaskay and *Power for Pemang* have both achieved widespread use in secondary schools and tertiary-education establishments in many different parts of the world. In addition to providing highly realistic case studies on the use of alternative-energy sources to generate electricity, they

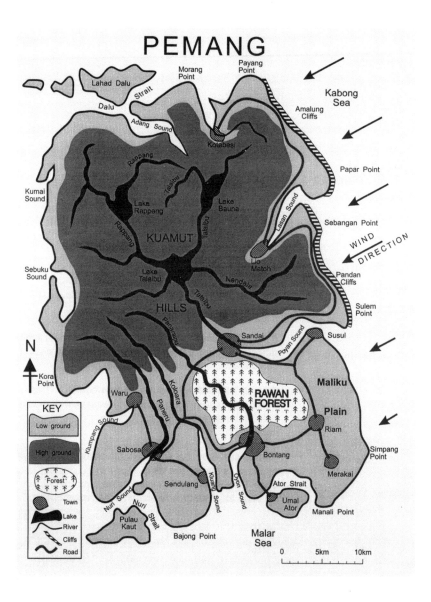

Figure 7.2 The map of the island on which *Power for Pemang* is based.

Group Worksheet – Hydroelectric Station

		Lake Rappang	Lake Bauna	Lake Talaibu
1.	Site of hydroelectric station			
2.	Catchment area of reservoir (sq. km)	50	70	220
3.	Average annual rainfall (mm)	3000	3000	3000
4.	Altitude of reservoir above sea-level (m)	250	270	130
5.	Effective operating head of scheme (m)	120	140	130
6.	Mass of water falling on catchment area of reservoir every year (million tonnes)	150	210	660
7.	Total potential energy that this represents (TJ)			
8.	Total number of kWh units of electricity produced by the station every year (millions)			
9.	Effective peak generating capacity of station (MW)			
10.	Capital cost of building dam (P$ millions)	20	30	35
11.	Capital cost of building tunnel between dam and generating station (P$ millions)	60	80	160
12.	Capital cost of generating station (P$ millions)	30	40	75
13.	Total capital cost of scheme (P$ millions)			
14.	Annual repayments/interest charges on loan taken out to meet capital costs (P$ millions)			
15.	Annual running and maintenance costs (P$ millions)	1.5	1.5	2.0
16.	Total annual costs (P$ millions)			
17.	Cost per unit of electricity produced (P$)			
18.	Cost per unit of electricity produced (cents)			

Figure 7.3 The worksheet completed by the group investigating the technical feasibility and economic viability of hydroelectric power.

COMPLETED Station Data Proforma

Type of scheme	Site(s) of scheme(s)	Annual electrical output of scheme (million kWh)	Peak output capacity of scheme (MW)	Time needed to build scheme (years)	Effective operational life of scheme (years)	Total capital cost of scheme (P$ millions)	Cost per unit of electricity produced by scheme (cents)
Wood-fired power station	West of Bontang, on shore of Oyon Sound	100 200	50 100	2 2	40 40	150 275	17.3 16.0
Combined solar/pumped storage scheme	Kuamut Hills near Lake Talaibu	100 200 300 400	100 200 300 400	3 3 3 3	25 25 25 25	753.3 1386.3 2009.7 2612.6	60.4 55.3 53.3 51.8
Combined wind/pumped storage scheme	Amalung Cliffs Pandan Cliffs Maliku Plain	35.0 16.0 7.6	17.0 8.0 4.0	3 3 3	50+ 50+ 50+	115 90 60	30.0 50.3 70.7
Combined tidal/pumped storage scheme	Adang Sound Ator Strait Sebuku Sound	225 133 65	106 62 30	4 4 4	50+ 50+ 50+	518 356 240	19.3 22.5 31.9
Hydroelectric scheme	Lake Rappang Lake Bauna Lake Talaibu	30 49 143	30 49 143	3 3 3	50+ 50+ 50+	110 150 270	33.7 26.9 16.2

Figure 7.4 The completed version of the proforma on which the participants record technical and economic data on the various possible schemes for generating electricity on Pemang.

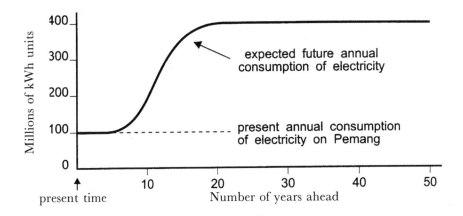

Figure 7.5 The demand curve that has to be met by the rolling programme for meeting Pemang's future electricity requirements.

help the participating pupils to develop a wide range of higher-cognitive skills (data processing, problem-solving, decision-making, planning, etc) and other useful transferable-process skills (eg communication skills, presentation skills, interpersonal skills, group and team skills). They also illustrate the conflicts of interest that often arise when technical projects are being planned, eg between economic and environmental considerations. The authors are convinced that complex, multi-stage simulations/games and case studies of this general type are among the most useful tools for developing higher-cognitive and transferable-process skills that are available to teachers working at upper-secondary and tertiary levels. The effort involved in organizing their use with a class is more than repaid in terms of the high quality of the learning that they help bring about. Try one if you have not already done so!

Developing communication, interpersonal and social skills

We have already seen how useful games and simulations can be in developing communication, interpersonal and social skills with nursery, primary and lower-secondary pupils. They are just as useful in developing such skills with older secondary pupils, and, increasingly, are being used to prepare such pupils to face the world of work.

Another reason for using games and simulations is that they are extremely useful vehicles to develop social and political awareness. A number of well-known exercises have been developed for this purpose at the Western Behavioral Institute in California, one of the most famous being *Starpower*. This can be used with pupils and students of any age over 10, being sufficiently flexible to adapt to a wide range of levels of ability and sophistication (one of the hallmarks of a really good game). It is, however, particularly useful at upper-secondary and tertiary levels. *Starpower* simulates the formation of a low-mobility, three-tiered trading society, and the almost inevitable subsequent exploitation of the 'have-nots' by the 'haves'. Its structure is shown in Figure 7.6, which also outlines the various activities that it incorporates. As can be seen, it consists of a series of cycles, each involving essentially the same activities.

Starpower is a fairly loosely structured exercise that depends almost entirely on flexible multi-way interaction of one form or another. First, there is the inter-player trading that takes place in the various plenary trading sessions – the activity on which the entire game is ultimately based. Second, there is the interaction that takes place *within* each of the three groups that emerge from the first round of trading. Third, there is the interaction that takes place *between* these three classes – interaction that eventually causes the game to break down when the 'upper class' (the squares) abuse their power by rewriting the rules in such a way that they make sure of conserving or increasing their position of privilege. This breakdown is, in fact, the ultimate object of the game (although the players do not know this), and, if it does not happen spontaneously – as it almost invariably does – the game controller takes steps to help it on its way by making appropriate secret suggestions to the squares. In the hands of a skilled, experienced controller (essential qualities if a potentially explosive exercise of this type is to run its course without degenerating into a real as opposed to a simulated conflict), the game and subsequent debriefing can be an extremely powerful educational tool as well as providing a memorable experience for the participants. Indeed, no one who takes part in a really lively session of *Starpower* is ever quite the same again!

Clearly, the debriefing that brings *Starpower* to a (hopefully) peaceful conclusion constitutes one of the most important parts of the exercise. It is here that the facilitator draws out the key lessons that the participants are expected to learn from their experience (the inherently unstable nature of a competitive society with no checks and balances, the tendency for a hierarchical class structure to develop spontaneously, the tendency of the resulting dominant class to take steps to secure and increase their dominance, the increasing tendency of the oppressed bottom class to rebel if their lot becomes manifestly intolerable, etc). Indeed, the debriefing can form the jumping-off point for a series of lessons – or an entire course – based on these various issues.

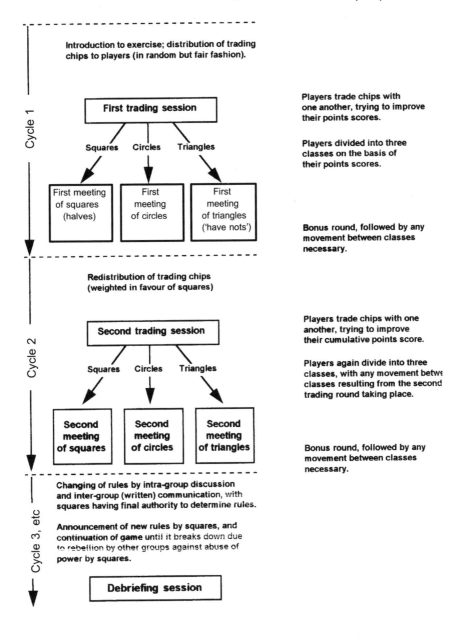

Introduction to exercise; distribution of trading chips to players (in random but fair fashion).

Cycle 1

First trading session

Squares   Circles   Triangles

| First meeting of squares (halves) | First meeting of circles | First meeting of triangles ('have nots') |

Players trade chips with one another, trying to improve their points scores.

Players divided into three classes on the basis of their points scores.

Bonus round, followed by any movement between classes necessary.

Redistribution of trading chips (weighted in favour of squares)

Cycle 2

Second trading session

Squares   Circles   Triangles

| Second meeting of squares | Second meeting of circles | Second meeting of triangles |

Players trade chips with one another, trying to improve their cumulative points score.

Players again divide into three classes, with any movement between classes resulting from the second trading round taking place.

Bonus round, followed by any movement between classes necessary.

Cycle 3, etc

Changing of rules by intra-group discussion and inter-group (written) communication, with squares having final authority to determine rules.

Announcement of new rules by squares, and continuation of game until it breaks down due to rebellion by other groups against abuse of power by squares.

Debriefing session

Figure 7.6 The schematic structure of *Starpower*.

Supplementing and supporting conventional laboratory work

Simulations and simulated case studies can also be used as a *supplement to*, and, in some cases as a *substitute for*, conventional laboratory work. Computer-based exercises are particularly useful in this role, and are enabling pupils and students to gain direct experience (through simulations) of a far wider range of experimental situations than was possible before such packages became available. They can, for example, enable pupils to learn how to control potentially dangerous plant such as chemical factories and nuclear reactors, carry out 'experiments' in otherwise inaccessible fields such as astrophysics, molecular biology and human genetics, and investigate situations where it is difficult or impracticable to carry out conventional laboratory experiments.

A good example of an exercise of the last type is a package on *Projectile Motion* that was developed by Eric Addinall and Henry Ellington for use at senior-secondary and lower-tertiary levels. Although conceptually simple, experiments on projectile motion are notoriously difficult to carry out in the laboratory. It was therefore decided to develop a simple computer simulation that would allow students to investigate the effects on the trajectory of a projectile that are produced by varying (a) the velocity of projection, (b) the angle of elevation of the initial motion, (c) the air resistance, and (d) the strength of the local gravitational field. Clearly, only (a) and (b) can easily be varied in a conventional laboratory situation, with (c) requiring a special pressure chamber and (d) being intrinsically impossible. By using a computer simulation, on the other hand, all four variables can be changed at will, allowing students to carry out a wide range of experiments whose results can then be compared with the predictions of standard theory. Use of the computer also enables the students to see the effect on the shape of the trajectory of changing the various parameters under their control – something that can never be properly achieved in a conventional experiment.

Computer simulations can also be used to enable pupils to 'try out' experiments before actually carrying them out in the laboratory. This is particularly useful in the teaching of electronics, where pupils can use packages such as *Electronics Workbench* to carry out preliminary design work on things like rectification circuits, filters, amplifiers, oscillators and radio receivers. Once they have done so, they can set up the actual circuit in the laboratory, and see how its performance compares with that of the simulated circuit. In this way, they can investigate any discrepancies between the two, and gain valuable insight into the difference between the theoretical performance of an ideal circuit and the actual performance of a real circuit. Computer-based design of this type is coming to play an increasingly important role in the teaching of a whole range of subjects at upper-secondary and tertiary levels.

Developing desirable attitudes and traits

Affective development, ie the development of desirable attitudes, values and behavioural traits, is an extremely important aspect of education at all levels. Appropriate use of games and simulations can again make a significant contribution to such development, as we have seen in Chapters 4–6, and the same is true at upper-secondary level. The *Starpower* simulation that was described earlier is one exercise that can be used in such a role, providing pupils with first-hand experience of what can happen to a society when one group is given too much power. The importance of thinking of the needs of others rather than simply looking after one's own vested interests is thus vividly brought home to the participants.

Exercises that place the participants in a situation where they have to look at complex problems or issues from different points of view are particularly effective in helping to develop desirable attitudes and values. A good example of an exercise of this type is *The Amsyn Problem*, one of a series of chemistry-based simulations/games and simulated case studies developed at Glasgow University for use in schools and colleges – see Figure 7.7.

The Amsyn Problem is based on the operations of 'Amsyn Ltd', a small chemical company that manufactures industrial chemicals known as aromatic amines. The company has operated successfully for many years, and has always enjoyed good relations with its workforce, the main problem being the pollution that it causes in the local river. Up to now, the company has got away with this, but the local district council is about to impose new, stricter regulations that will make it necessary for the company to make drastic changes to its method of operation or face the prospect of closure. The game involves three groups of pupils, representing groups with completely different vested interests, looking at the problem from their own particular points of view and formulating their preferred solutions. The first group represents the Amsyn management, whose main priority is to ensure that the company continues to operate – and continues to make a profit. The second represents the Amsyn workers, whose main priority is to ensure that no jobs are lost (some possible solutions would result in a drastic reduction in the workforce). The third represents the local district council, whose main priority is to ensure that their new regulations are fully complied with. The central part of the game consists of a meeting at which these three groups come together to discuss the problem faced by the company, and see whether a solution that would be acceptable to all parties can be found. (It can, given a little ingenuity and willingness to compromise on the part of the different groups.)

At one level, *The Amsyn Problem* is simply a highly realistic case study in applied chemistry and chemical engineering. At another, deeper level it is a

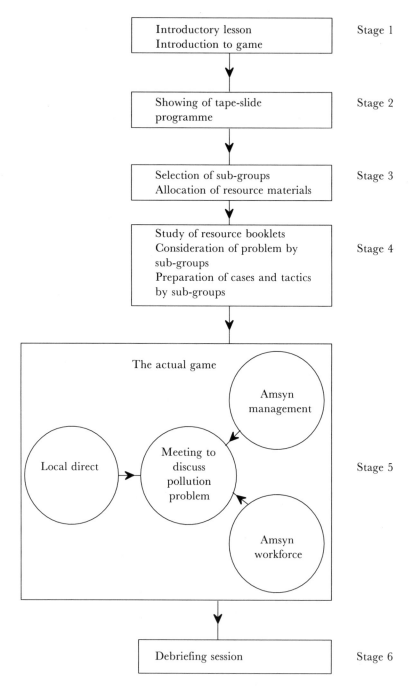

Figure 7.7 The schematic structure of *The Amsyn Problem*.

powerful vehicle for helping to achieve a whole range of important affective objectives – making the participants realize that real-life problems can be viewed from different, often conflicting perspectives, making them willing to listen to, and take account of, other people's points of view, demonstrating the importance of creative thinking and compromise, and so on. The authors are again fully convinced of the great educational value of such exercises.

Developing multi-faceted skills relating to real life

Pupils in the upper forms of secondary schools and tertiary-level students can use games and simulations to develop the various multi-faceted, work-related skills that they will require once they enter employment. They can, for example, be taught office skills in simulated office situations, business skills by running simulated businesses, and catering skills by working in simulated hotels and restaurants. Indeed, many schools and colleges now operate highly realistic training restaurants that provide training in virtually all aspects of such work – ordering raw materials, cooking the food, serving it to customers, and so on.

A good example of a multi-faceted business game is the *Bruce Oil Management Game*, a computer-based simulation/game based on the development of an offshore oilfield that was originally developed in Robert Gordon's Institute of Technology during the 1970s. This was run annually as a national (later an international) competition for school, college and business teams for several years, and was also used for over 20 years as an exercise for business management, offshore engineering and mathematics students. Games of this type help the participants to develop an extremely wide range of work-related skills, and are an excellent preparation for real life.

Detailed case study

Let us end this chapter by taking a detailed look at how games and simulations were built into a major curriculum-development project in one particular secondary school – the Gordon Schools, Huntly. The project (known as *Oil Strike Huntly*) was the brainchild of Bernard Brown, Grampian Region's Schools/Industry Liaison Officer, and involved the whole of the senior school (S4, S5 and S6), whose normal timetable was suspended for an entire week in June 1984 so that all the pupils could take part.

The Project was built round a highly realistic simulation of a *public inquiry* – the process whereby a controversial major development is subjected to public scrutiny and debate in Britain. This particular public inquiry was called to consider an application by Britannia Oil plc (an imaginary oil company) to develop a small onshore oilfield that they had 'discovered' near Huntly – a small town roughly 40 miles NW of Aberdeen – three years earlier. Following the drilling of a number of appraisal wells, it had been estimated that the field contained roughly 15 million barrels of recoverable oil, and that the production potential over its 12-year life would be between 4000 and 7000 barrels a day. A detailed planning application for the development of the Huntly Field had been submitted to Gordon District Council (the local authority responsible for dealing with such planning applications). A number of objections had been raised, however, so a full public inquiry into the proposed development had been scheduled to take place on Thursday, 21 June–Friday, 22 June 1984.

The project was meticulously planned, the detailed scenario on the proposed Huntly Field development being prepared with the help of the Environmental Services Department at BP's Exploration and Production Headquarters in Aberdeen. Help on the planning of the public inquiry itself was received from Gordon District Council and a local legal firm, with many other organizations and individuals giving advice on specific aspects of the project. The school set up a simulated 'newspaper', a simulated 'radio station' and a simulated 'TV station' to provide coverage of the project, and received extensive help on their planning and organization from the 'real' local newspaper, radio station and TV company. The project also received financial support from the Department of Trade and Industry, who saw it as an excellent vehicle for promoting school–industry liaison in the NE of Scotland.

The timetable for the entire week of the project was as follows.

Monday, 18 June (am)
Meeting of Britannia Oil plc to discuss their strategy for the public inquiry.
Simulated public meeting to provide a forum for open discussion of the proposed development, with an associated exhibition.

Monday, 18 June (pm)
Briefing for 'barristers' who would be representing Britannia Oil and the other main groups who would be presenting evidence at the public inquiry.

Tuesday, 19 June (am)
Private meetings of various groups who would be presenting evidence, to prepare their cases.

Tuesday, 19 June (pm)
Simulated meeting of local District Council to discuss its attitude to the proposed development.

Wednesday, 20 June (all day)
Making and 'broadcasting' of radio and television programmes on the proposed development, involving all interested parties.

Thursday, 21 June (am)
All written submissions by groups wishing to be represented at public inquiry had to be completed and submitted by 11 am.

11 am: Concert given by visiting School of Performing and Vocal Arts, Houston, Texas.
Thursday, 21 June (pm)
First open session of public inquiry held in School Hall.
Friday, 22 June (am)
Second open session of public inquiry held in School Hall.
Friday, 22 June (pm)
Public inquiry 'Reporter' (Mr Bill Goodland, of Grampian Regional Council) gave his decision on the proposed planning application.
Plenary debriefing and evaluation session on exercise, involving all coordinators, group advisers, participating pupils and visitors.
Monday, 25 June
Local 'newspaper' (*Huntly Herald*) carried post-inquiry features and news.

The simulated public inquiry that formed the heart of the *Oil Strike Huntly* project was conducted in exactly the same way as a real public inquiry in Scotland. It was chaired by a 'Reporter' appointed by the Secretary of State for Scotland (Bill Goodland), and all the main parties were represented by 'barristers'. The inquiry opened with a presentation on behalf of Britannia Oil, which highlighted the positive aspects of the proposal (the jobs that it would generate, the wealth that it would bring to the area, etc) and tried to draw the teeth of the opposition by assuring them that the harmful effects on the environment would be minimal. A number of local businesses then made presentations supporting the proposed development, claiming that it would stimulate the economy of the region. The main opposition came from the local Residents' Association and the conservation lobby, who felt that any benefits that the development might bring would be far outweighed by the harmful effects on the local community (pressure on housing, loss of valuable agricultural land, increase in crime, etc) and on the environment (the visual impact of the site, the damage to an area of special scientific interest, and so on). The arguments continued for a total of six hours, and, despite the persuasiveness of the opposition's arguments, the Reporter eventually ruled in favour of the developers (they usually do!). He did, however, insist that the site of special scientific interest should be safeguarded.

In terms of its sheer scale and complexity, *Oil Strike Huntly* was one of the largest and most ambitious simulation/game projects ever to take place in a Scottish secondary school. The educational benefits to the participating pupils were many and wide-ranging. First and foremost, they gained an insight into the social role and method of operation of public inquiries that they could never have obtained through conventional teaching, and also learned a great deal about many other aspects of local government and industrial and commercial activity. The realism of the project was particularly impressive. The location of the proposed oil development was real, and the pupils could (and did) go and look at it. The scenario was more than credible, having been meticulously designed and planned with the aid of experts from BP. The submissions to the public inquiry were based on professional advice, and, as we have seen, the public inquiry itself was an extremely accurate simulation of the real thing. It is impossible to list all the different skills that the project helped the participating pupils to develop, which included research skills, communication skills of all types, media skills, team skills, and interpersonal and social skills. One of the authors (Henry Ellington) was privileged to observe the project (he actually played a minor role – as an 'expert witness' at the public inquiry). He came away extremely impressed by what he had seen, and was more than ever convinced of the great power and effectiveness of large-scale simulations and games as educational tools.

In subsequent years, Bernard Brown organized local versions of the same basic project in a number of other Grampian secondary schools, always with the same success that was achieved at Huntly. A simulated public inquiry of this type can be based on *any* controversial local development – the opening of a new quarry or mine, the building of a factory that is likely to cause pollution, the construction of a new road, and so on. Any readers who are interested in organizing a project of this type should get in touch with Bernard Brown, who has now retired from his post as Grampian's School/ Industry Liaison Officer but would be happy to act as a consultant to the organizers. He can be contacted through any of the authors.

Table 7.1 Model solution to exercise shown in Figure 7.1.

Name of field	Uniform	Victor	Whisky	X-ray	Yankee	Zulu
Ranking as an investment prospect	2	4	3	1	5	6
Overall assessment as an investment prospect	good	good	good	good	marginal	bad

8

Designing Your Own Exercises
The 'Top-Down' Approach

Having completed our detailed examination of how games and simulations can be used with different ages of pupil, we will now take a look at how to set about designing your own exercises. In this chapter we will describe one possible approach to such work – the 'top-down' or 'algorithmic' approach.

The algorithmic approach to game design

If you cannot find an existing game or simulation that can be used with your pupils as it stands, or can be modified to meet your specific needs, you can, of course, always try to produce your own custom-designed exercise. Several books have been written on how to do so, the authors generally advocating some sort of 'algorithmic' approach that involves working systematically through a clearly defined series of steps. Such an approach was in fact recommended by one of the authors (Henry Ellington) in the books on game design that he wrote with Eric Addinall and Fred Percival during the 1980s (see Further Reading). This approach, which was subsequently incorporated in the 'do-it-yourself' kit on game design that Joannie Fowlie and Henry Ellington produced for use in Grampian schools, involves the following three stages:

1. Establishing the *basic design criteria*.
2. Formulating the *basic idea* for the exercise.
3. Converting the basic idea into a *viable educational package*.

Let us now look at each of these stages in more detail.

Stage 1 Establishing the basic design criteria

The starting point of the design process should always be the question: 'Why do you want to design an exercise of the game/simulation/case-study type?' In the case of an exercise that is being designed for educational purposes, the question generally involves asking two further questions, namely, 'With what specific group(s) of pupils or students is the exercise to be used?' and 'What specific educational objectives do you want to achieve?' In other words, it involves establishing the *basic design criteria* of the exercise in terms of its *target population* and *design objectives*.

Once you have established your design criteria, you should take a critical look at these and ask yourself whether an exercise of the game/simulation/case-study type is likely to be the most effective way of achieving the sort of objectives you have in mind for your pupils or students. In other words, what can a game, simulation or case study achieve that more conventional teaching methods cannot? Unless there is some distinct advantage to be gained by using such an exercise, then there is little point in proceeding further.

Stage 2 Formulating the basic idea for the exercise

Assuming that you have worked systematically through all the above processes, and have established that a clear need for a new exercise exists, you can now move on to the first stage of the design process itself – formulating the *basic idea* for your exercise. This should itself be tackled in the following three stages.

1 Choosing the CONTENT of the exercise

The first step in the process is to decide (in general terms) what the *content* of the exercise should be. In many cases, this will follow more or less directly from the design criteria, particularly in the case of exercises where the desired outcomes are mainly cognitive in nature (ie deal with the learning, application, use or evaluation of facts or principles of some sort). Suppose, for example, that you are a chemistry teacher who wants to produce an exercise designed to help your students understand a particular set of chemical reactions; you would almost certainly choose these reactions as the subject matter of your exercise, as did the designers of the *Formulon* and *Chemsyn* card games that will be described in detail in Chapter 9.

In other cases, however, the choice of content may not be quite so straightforward. Indeed, the content of an exercise of the game or simulation type is often only a foundation on which a structure capable of achieving the desired design outcomes may be built. This is particularly so in the case of exercises where the main object is to help the participants develop broad-based skills of one form or another, eg problem-solving, decision-making, interpersonal, communication or general process skills, or to help them develop desirable attitudinal traits, eg a willingness to appreciate the points of view of other people. A designer wishing to develop an exercise for such purposes could base it on virtually any suitable subject matter relevant to the group with which it is to be used. However, exercises of this type turn out to be particularly useful if they are designed to 'kill two birds with one stone', ie if they use a content that is of intrinsic value and interest to the participants as a vehicle for achieving these wider objectives. The *Power for Pemang* and *Amsyn Problem* simulation/games described in Chapter 7 are good examples of multi-purpose exercises of this type.

2 Choosing the FORMAT for the exercise

Once a possible content for the exercise has been identified, the next step should be to choose a suitable *format*. Here are some of the main options:

- a *simple manual* exercise, ie an exercise that does not involve the use of special resource materials (such as packs of cards or boards) or specialized equipment (such as a computer), only simple, easy-to-produce materials such as role cards, briefing sheets or booklets
- a *card game*, ie a game that involves the use of a specially designed pack (or packs) of cards
- a *board game*, ie a game played on a specially designed surface of some sort
- a *computer-based exercise*, ie one that involves the use of an external computer, PC or network.

When choosing the format for your exercise, your aim should be to decide which of the various possible formats would be best suited to achieve your selected design outcomes, using the content that you have provisionally selected, and bearing in mind the production constraints of your individual situation. Obviously, your own experience and individual preference will play an important role in reaching this decision, and it is strongly recommended that you limit yourself to formats with which you will be able to work with confidence. There is little point, for example, in trying to produce a computer-based exercise if you cannot programme or do not have access to a suitable authoring system, unless, of course, you can enlist the help of a colleague who has the necessary IT skills.

In many cases, it will be found that one particular format is more suitable than any of the others for achieving the aims you have in mind. If you are trying to develop interpersonal skills, for example, you will probably find that some sort of simple manual, role-playing exercise would best meet your needs. In other cases, however, more than one format may be equally suitable and, in this event, it is probably advisable to opt for the format that will produce the simplest possible exercise capable of meeting your basic design requirements. Do not, for example, decide to produce a complex multi-strategy exercise or a sophisticated computer simulation if a simple card game or role-playing exercise would meet your needs equally effectively.

3 Deciding on the OVERALL STRUCTURE of the exercise

Once you have selected the format in which your exercise is to be produced, your choice of possible structures will automatically be restricted to those that can be used with that particular format. Let us therefore take a look at the range of *structures* that is possible with each of the main formats that were identified in the previous section.

Simple manual exercises

Exercises of this type can have an extremely wide range of structures. Some have a simple structure that is effectively defined by the type of basic activity that the exercise involves, eg solving a problem, or taking part in some form of role-play. In others, the structure is more complicated, constituting an overall organizational framework within which the various activities that the exercise involves take place. Most exercises of the latter type are found to fall into five basic classes:

1. *Linear structures,* ie structures in which the participants work systematically through the same essentially linear programme of activities. Such structures are extremely useful in situations where a complicated case study or procedure has to be broken down into easily manageable stages, and are particularly suitable for developing high-level cognitive skills. A typical linear structure is shown schematically in Figure 8.1, the *North Sea Auction* simulation/game described in Chapter 3 being a good example of an exercise with such a basic structure.

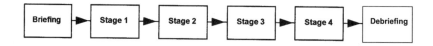

Figure 8.1 A typical 'linear' structure.

2. *Radial structures,* ie structures in which each participant (or group of
    participants) first carries out a set of preparatory activities specific to a
    given role in a scenario or point of view in a problem situation, and then
    presents information or argues a case at a plenary session or simulated
    meeting of some sort. Radial structures are particularly well suited for
    use in complex role-playing situations such as simulated meetings, public
    inquiries, etc. They are ideal for developing communication and
    interpersonal skills, and for achieving affective objectives. A typical
    'radial' structure is shown schematically in Figure 8.2, the *Amsyn Problem*
    simulation/game described in Chapter 7 being an example of an exercise
    with an essentially radial structure.

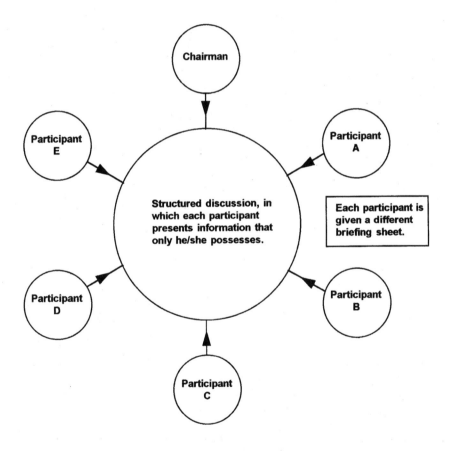

Figure 8.2 A typical 'radial' structure.

3. *Cyclic structures*, ie structures in which the activities take place in a repetitive series of cycles, such as a series of decision-making/data processing/feedback cycles, as shown schematically in Figure 8.3. Such structures are widely used in business games and computer simulations. The *Bruce Oil Management Game* described in Chapter 7 is a good example of an exercise with a cyclic structure of this type; this involved working through six successive decision-making/data processing/feedback cycles.

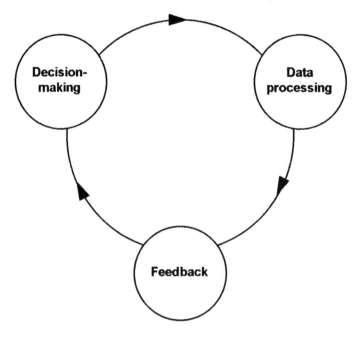

Figure 8.3 A typical 'cyclic' structure.

4. *Interactive structures*, in which the most important organizational feature is some form of multi-way interaction between individuals or groups. The interaction can take a variety of forms, eg exchange of information, trading, negotiation, lobbying, and can be organized in a large number of ways, but almost invariably makes the resulting exercise 'looser', less formal and less predictable than tightly-structured exercises of the linear, radial or cyclic type. Such structures are ideal for simulating complex social, organizational, political and international situations, and for the investigation of group dynamics. They are also useful for developing communication and interpersonal skills and for achieving affective objectives. A typical interactive structure is shown schematically in Figure 8.4, the *Barter* simulation/game described in Chapter 6 being a good example of an exercise with this type of structure.

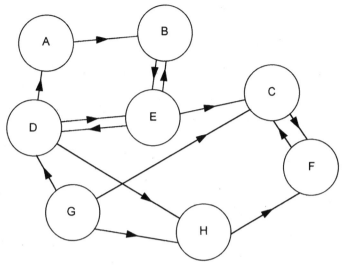

Figure 8.4 A typical 'interactive' structure.

5. *Composite structures*, ie structures that incorporate two or more of the 'simple' structures described above. The *Power for Pemang* and *Starpower* simulations/games described in Chapter 7 are good examples of exercises with such composite structures. As shown in Figure 7.6, the latter incorporates a series of interactive structures of different types within an overall cyclic structure. A typical composite structure is shown schematically in Figure 8.5.

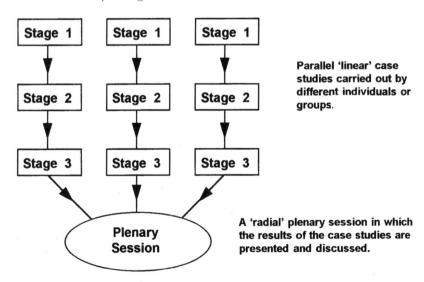

Figure 8.5 A typical 'composite' structure.

Card games

Here at least four basic types of structure can be used.

1. The *bridge, whist* class of structures, in which each participant is dealt a hand of cards and then has to play these individually in order to win tricks.
2. The *pontoon, poker, rummy* class of structures, in which the participants have to build up winning patterns or sequences using the cards they have been dealt and acquire during play.
3. The *Happy Families, snap* class of structures, in which the participants have to collect as many cards as possible from their opponents, or from a common pool.
4. The *patience, solitaire* class of structures, in which a single player has to arrange a pack (or set) of cards into a pattern of some sort.

These different structures will all be examined in greater detail in Chapter 9.

Board games

Here, there are again at least four basic types of structure that can be used.

1. The *Scrabble, go* class of structures, in which the board serves as a two-dimensional matrix on which static patterns or structures can be built up.
2. The *Monopoly, Ludo, Snakes and Ladders* class of structures, in which the board is used to provide a pre-determined linear path (or pattern of paths) along or around which players have to progress.
3. The *chess* class of structures, in which the board serves as a field for mobile, two-dimensional play.
4. *Composite* structures, which combine two or more of the above basic structures, eg using movement round a *Monopoly*-type perimeter circuit to control pattern-building or two-dimensional activities in the interior.

These different structures will all be examined in greater detail in Chapter 9.

Computer-based exercises

Here, a vast range of different structures can be used, five of the basic ones being listed below.

1. *Linear structures*, similar to those described for simple manual exercises.
2. *Branching structures*, where the path that a participant takes through the exercise is determined by decisions made or performance of tasks, as in a branching programme in programmed learning.
3. *Cyclic structures*, similar to those described for simple manual exercises.
4. *Two-dimensional structures*, in which the field of a VDU screen is used for two-dimensional pattern building, two-dimensional play, etc.

5. *Composite structures*, ie complex structures that incorporate two or more of the 'simple' structures described above and create an 'open' learning environment.

When choosing a structure for an exercise, you are strongly advised to explore the possibilities of using one of the 'standard' structures appropriate to the format in which you will be working before trying to think up a completely new structure all by yourself. You will probably find that one of these is suitable for your purposes, thus saving you a great deal of time and effort. (The next chapter will provide further guidelines on how to do this.)

Stage 3 Converting the basic idea into a viable educational package

Once you have developed what you think is a sound basic idea for a new exercise, the next task that confronts you is the conversion of this basic idea into a viable package of materials that can be used for the purpose you have in mind. This should again be tackled in three separate stages:

1. Deciding on the overall form of the package.
2. Producing a prototype package.
3. Field-testing and revising the package.

Deciding on the overall form of the package

The first stage in the conversion process is to decide what the *overall form* of the package should be. Whatever type of exercise is to be produced, the package will include the following basic components:

- any specialized materials that the participants will need in order to take part in the exercise
- a set of instructions on how to run or take part in the exercise, eg in the form of an organizer's guide or participants' manual.

The detailed form of the package will obviously depend on the format and overall structure that have been selected for the exercise. Typically, they will be along the following lines.

Simple manual exercises
- an organizer's guide of some sort (if appropriate)
- a participants' guide of some sort, eg a set of rules or instructional manual (if appropriate)
- any introductory material thought necessary, eg an introductory sheet or booklet

- any resource materials needed by the participants (role sheets, briefing sheets, etc).

Card games
- an organizer's guide of some sort (if appropriate)
- a participants' guide of some sort, eg as a set of rules or a game manual
- a pack (or set of packs) of appropriate cards.

Board games
- an organizer's guide of some sort (if appropriate)
- a participants' guide of some sort, eg a set of rules or game manual
- a suitably designed board
- any ancillary materials needed to play the game (playing pieces, tokens, sets of cards, sets of money, dice, etc).

Computer-based exercises
- an organizer's guide of some sort (if appropriate)
- a user's or participants' guide of some sort (if needed)
- the computer program(s) needed to run the exercise
- any ancillary materials needed, eg worksheets.

Producing a prototype package

The next stage in the development of a viable educational package is the design and production of all the various materials that will be needed. Here, the best advice that can be offered to would-be designers is this: try to find an existing exercise that has a similar format and structure to what you are wanting to produce and then base your own materials on its resource materials. Remember Tom Lehrer's immortal advice to those wishing to achieve success in mathematics: 'Plagiarize!' (The next chapter will provide further guidelines on how to do this.)

When developing the resource materials for a game, simulation or case study, it is important to make sure that each item:

- is capable of fulfilling its own specific function
- fits into the general context of the exercise
- is consistent with all the other materials in the package.

This will almost certainly involve a certain amount of 'tuning', ie revising or amending particular items as the work progresses in order to produce a self-consistent, balanced package. This stage of the development process can be thought of as a 'black box' into which you feed the basic idea for the exercise and out of which eventually emerges a prototype educational package. Just what goes on inside the black box will depend on a wide range of factors – the type of exercise being produced, the working style of the designer, and so on. Greatly simplified schematic representations of the process for each of the four basic classes of exercise being considered – simple manual exercises, card games, board games and computer-based exercises – are given in Figures 8.6, 8.7, 8.8 and 8.9. These diagrams identify the main elements that must be considered in each case, and give a rough idea of what goes on inside the black box.

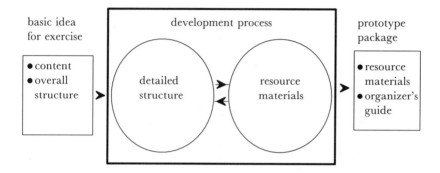

Figure 8.6 Development of a simple manual exercise.

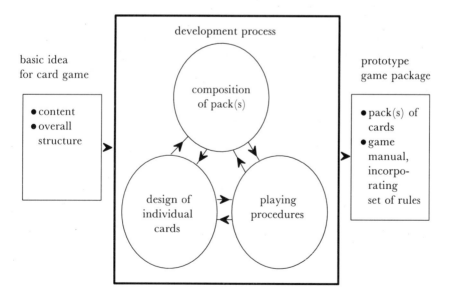

Figure 8.7 Development of a card game.

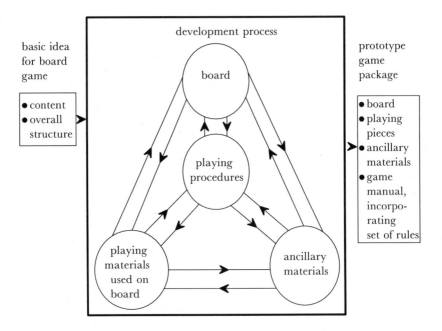

Figure 8.8 Development of a board game.

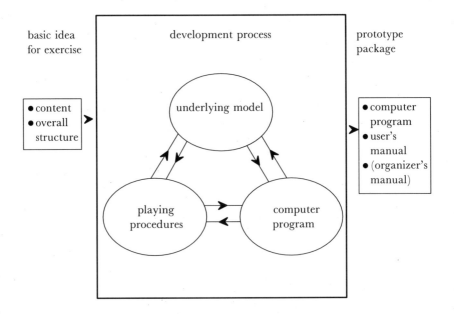

Figure 8.9 Development of a computer-based exercise.

Whatever the format and structure of the exercise, your primary aim should always be to produce a package of materials that can be used not only by yourself but also by others wishing to use the exercise. For this reason, it is essential to include in the participants' guide or user's manual and (if one is included) the organizer's guide *all* the information needed to take part in or use the exercise effectively. Never be afraid to spell out in detail what might (to you) appear to be obvious; it might not be quite so obvious to someone who has never seen the exercise before. Further information on how to write an organizer's guide is given in Chapter 3.

Field-testing and revising the package

The third step in the development of a viable educational package is the process by which it is field tested in order to determine whether it is (a) logistically and operationally sound, and (b) capable of achieving its design objectives. The package is then revised or amended in the light of the feedback obtained.

The first full-scale field test of a package (as opposed to 'dry runs' carried out by the designer during the development of the package materials) is an extremely important stage in the development process. It should be organized and supervised by the designer, and, if possible, should be run with a group of people drawn from (or similar to) the target population. Such a field trial can have a number of possible outcomes:

1. The exercise turns out to be a complete disaster, either from an organizational or from a logistical point of view, or (equally important) from the point of view of its design objectives. This indicates that the designer has obviously not got things right, and that the whole concept should be critically re-examined and the exercise either abandoned or drastically modified.

2. The exercise proves successful in some respects but less so in others, revealing a number of basic (but not disastrous) flaws in the design. Surprising as it may seem, this is an extremely satisfactory outcome from the designer's point of view, since it:

   (a) shows that the basic idea appears to be sound
   (b) identifies those areas where some modification is required
   (c) (hopefully) gives some clues as to what these modifications should be.

   Needless to say, all such changes, whether relating to the overall form of the package, to the detailed contents of the resource materials, or to the method of play or organizational procedure, should be made before any further field tests are attempted.

3. The exercise proves to be completely successful in all respects, apart from comparatively minor points of detail which can be remedied without a major re-write. This is even more satisfactory (albeit unlikely!), and indicates that the exercise can be safely handed over to colleagues for further, more rigorous field testing. Any weaknesses identified by these further tests should obviously also be remedied.

Making an exercise generally available to the educational community

Let us assume that you have satisfactorily completed all the above stages of the design process, and have finally produced an exercise that appears to meet all its design criteria. You may well now be content to 'call it a day', and simply use the exercise for whatever purpose it was designed. You may, on the other hand, want to take the development process one stage further, and make your exercise generally available to your colleagues in the educational community. All too often, a very promising new exercise that could be of real use to teachers throughout the country never achieves its full potential because the designer fails to take this final step.

There are three ways in which you can make a new exercise generally available:

- by developing a suitable 'do-it-yourself' kit for producing the package
- by producing and distributing full sets of the package yourself
- by having the package produced and distributed by an appropriate publisher.

Let us now examine each of these in greater detail.

Producing a 'do-it-yourself' kit

This is perhaps the simplest and cheapest way of making an exercise more generally available. The contents of the kit will depend very much on the format of the exercise and the nature of the materials that compose the package, but should always include the following:

- detailed instructions on how to produce *all* the materials needed to use or run the exercise, including, where appropriate, photocopy masters of any documents required by the participants
- a copy of the user's manual and/or organizer's guide.

In the case of card or board games, where it is generally extremely time-consuming to produce multiple sets and can be difficult to find an external publisher willing to take on the exercise, production of a 'do-it-yourself' kit of this type is often the best way to publish the exercise. If you do decide to publish in this way, remember to include a statement giving users copyright clearance to make multiple copies of any relevant documents, otherwise they may be breaking the law by so doing.

'Do-it-yourself' kits can, of course, also be published electronically – either on floppy disk or CD-ROM, or by making them available via the Internet. The latter is being increasingly used for disseminating educational materials of all types.

Producing multiple sets of a package

In the case of simple manual exercises, where all the resource materials can be run off on a photocopier, this can again be an extremely cost-effective way of making an exercise generally available. All you need is a clean set of photocopy masters of all the various documents that are included in the package and, of course, access to a good, fast photocopier capable of handling a large throughput. Sets of the package can then be run off in whatever numbers are required, and (if appropriate) sold at a price sufficient to cover the cost of production, postage and overheads – plus any profit margin that you want to build in. Many highly successful educational packages have been published in this way.

Full sets of many game/simulation/case-study packages can again be made available electronically – either via floppy disk, CD-ROM or via the Internet.

Publication by an appropriate body

If a suitable publisher can be found, this is by far the most satisfactory method of making an exercise generally available, since it relieves the designer of all the problems associated with mass-production and distribution. It also generally results in a final product of much higher quality.

In the case of educational packages of the game/simulation/case-study type, possible publishers include:

- your own school, college or local education authority, which may well be prepared to publish a worthwhile exercise, eg through its central resources centre or curriculum-development centre, or via its commercial activities unit, if it has one
- an appropriate professional body or official organization such as the Association for Science Education, College Lane, Hatfield, Herts AL10 9AA, and its equivalents in other subject areas
- a commercial publishing house that already publishes packages of a similar type; try Kogan Page, 120 Pentonville Road, London N1 9JN.

If you want to make any money out of the publication of your exercise, a commercial publisher is obviously your best bet, if you can persuade one to take your 'baby' on board!

9

Designing Your Own Exercises
The 'Bottom-Up' Approach

This chapter looks at a somewhat simpler and highly practical approach to the design of classroom games and simulations – the 'bottom-up' or 'inspirational' approach.

The inspirational approach to game design

As we saw in the last chapter, most authors of books and manuals on game design advocate some sort of 'algorithmic' approach involving working through a prescribed series of steps in a logical, systematic way. Such an approach has been found to work extremely well in practice, and is probably the best way in which to tackle the design of certain types of exercise – large-scale role-playing simulation/games and interactive case studies, for example.

When designing board games, card games and other manual games for use in the classroom, however, there is another, somewhat less complicated, approach that can be adopted. Although this might not meet with the approval of the 'systems approach' purists, it does appear to work extremely well for most people who try it. It involves simply looking at the range of board, card and other games that are available in the shops or are played by families at home and seeing if any of these might be used as the basis of an educational game of some sort. This chapter has been written to help teachers, particularly those working in nursery and primary schools, to adopt this 'bottom-up' approach to the design of classroom games. It does so by examining the main paradigms on which board, card and other manual 'fun' games are based and identifying some of the ways in which they might be used for educational purposes. It also presents detailed case studies on how this can be done, drawn mainly from the authors' own experience of educational game design. The chapter ends by presenting some general pointers on how to make effective use of the approach.

Some useful paradigms for educational board games

Board games come in many different forms, but it is possible to identify a few basic paradigms that underlie the design of the great majority. Let us now take a look at some of the most important of these and examine their possible educational applications.

The Scrabble, go paradigm

In games of this general type, the board serves as a matrix on which static patterns of some sort are progressively built up as play proceeds, players generally taking turns to add pieces or elements to the resulting pattern. Such games can vary enormously in complexity, sophistication and difficulty, depending on the nature of the pattern building involved. They can be used for a wide range of educational purposes, eg to reinforce the teaching of basic facts and principles and to develop higher-cognitive skills relating to such things as decision-making and forward-planning. Like most board, card and other manual games, they can also be used to help the participants develop spoken-communication and interpersonal skills – something that can be particularly useful with younger pupils (with all the other paradigms to be discussed in this chapter, we will take this 'as read' in order to avoid repetition).

Illustrative example

A typical example of this genre is *Lebensraum*, another of the simulation/games developed for use in teaching the 'Environment' section of the Scottish Foundation and General Level Science Curriculum during the 1980s. The layout of the board used in this game is shown in Figure 9.1.

The game simulates the process whereby rival species compete for territory in a limited area such as an island, and is played in much the same way as *go*, using tokens with one black and one white face. The players representing the two species take it in turns to place one of their tokens on a 'hex', the object being to occupy as much territory as possible. The only complicating factor is that a 'confined colony' which has no room into which to expand and fails to reach the critical size of seven can be over-run by the other species, by having its tokens turned over; it is this factor that makes the game interesting and fun to play.

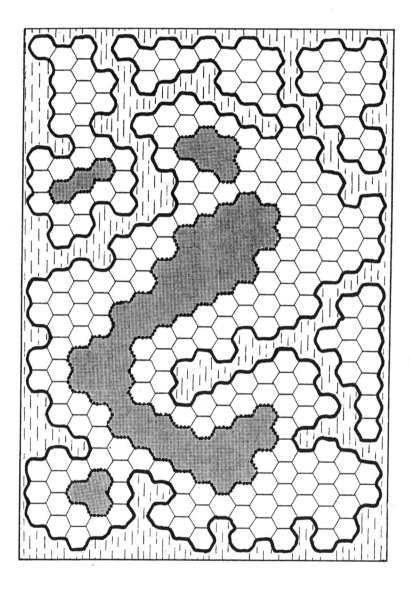

Figure 9.1 The layout of the board used in *Lebensraum*.

The snakes and ladders, ludo *paradigm*

In this class of game, the board constitutes an essentially 'linear' race track (or combination of linear race tracks) along which players have to move in some prescribed way, movement generally being controlled by throwing a die (or, in some cases, a pair of dice). Such games tend to be fairly simple, their main educational applications being the reinforcement of the teaching of basic facts and principles and (in some cases) attitude formation.

Illustrative examples

A typical example is *Health Snakes and Ladders*, a simple game that was developed for use in teaching the 'Healthy Bodies' section of the Scottish Foundation and General Level Science Curriculum (see Figure 9.2). The game is played in exactly the same way as ordinary *snakes and ladders*, the main educational aim being to reinforce teaching that some practices are 'good' for you, while others are 'bad' – and that they also vary considerably in terms of the amount of good or harm they can do you. The board is (it is to be hoped) self-explanatory.

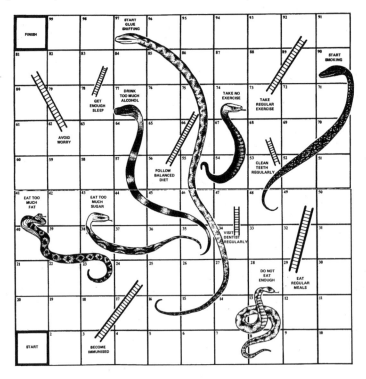

Figure 9.2 The board used in *Health Snakes and Ladders*.

The *Road Safety Ludo* board game described in Chapter 5 is another good example of a 'linear race' game of this type, this time based on the ludo model. The layout of the board used in this game is shown in Figure 5.8. The game is designed to reinforce teaching on road safety at lower-primary level.

The chess, Chinese Checkers *paradigm*

Here, the board is used as a vehicle for mobile, two-dimensional conflict or race-type activity of some sort. Games based on this paradigm can again vary enormously in complexity, sophistication and difficulty, and (like pattern-building games) can be used for a wide range of educational purposes – reinforcing the teaching of basic facts and principles, developing decision-making and forward-planning skills, and so on.

Illustrative example

A good example of a classroom game based on this paradigm is *Microbe Attack*. This is another game that was developed for teaching the 'Healthy Bodies' section of the Scottish Foundation and General Level Science Curriculum. It can be played on an ordinary draughts (checkers) or chess board using a 'crown' to represent a microbe that is trying to invade the body and four ordinary pieces to represent 'killer' blood cells that are trying to trap and destroy it. The 'microbe' starts on a black square at the top of the board, with the four 'killer cells' on the black squares at the bottom; the former can move both backwards and forwards, whereas the latter can only move forwards, movement being restricted to the black squares in both cases. If the microbe breaks through the defensive line of killer cells, it wins, and infects the body; if the killer cells trap it against the sides or top of the board, they win. The game is a simple simulation of the process by which the human body protects itself against bacterial infection, being designed to reinforce teaching of this topic in an enjoyable way.

The Monopoly *paradigm*

This is the paradigm that has by far the largest number of educational applications, since the dice-controlled movement round the perimeter can be used:

- to control game-related activities *on* the actual board
- to control game-related activities *off* the surface of the board
- to control real-life activities of some sort.

All three modes can be used to achieve a wide range of lower-cognitive objectives (reinforcement of knowledge and understanding), higher-cognitive objectives (application of principles, analysis, decision-making, problem-solving, forward planning, etc) and affective objectives (reinforcement of desirable attitudes and values). The third mode can also be a powerful vehicle for developing psychomotor skills.

Illustrative examples

Several classroom games based on the *Monopoly* paradigm have been described earlier in this book, and readers are referred to these for illustrative examples of the genre. These include:

- the *Class Tuck Shop Game* described in Chapter 5 (see Figure 5.6); this is designed to help lower-primary pupils develop their basic counting and money-handling skills
- the *Towie Shortbread Game* described in Chapter 5 (see detailed case study at end of chapter); this used *Monopoly*-type movement round the perimeter of the board to control the process by which early-primary children *actually made* shortbread in the class
- the *Shortbread Process* game also described in the detailed case study at the end of Chapter 5; this was designed to help the pupils gain an insight into the nature of the bakery business, particularly related to costs and profits
- the *Culraggie Whisky Game* described in Chapter 6 (see Figure 6.5); this was designed to give older primary pupils an insight into the commercial manufacture of whisky
- the *Contract 3-5* game described in the detailed case study in Chapter 6 (see Figure 6.8); this was designed to help older primary pupils gain a better understanding of commercial contracts.

Between them, these five games illustrate all three of the basic modes of the *Monopoly* paradigm that are outlined above.

The Trivial Pursuit *paradigm*

Although it is broadly based on the *Monopoly* paradigm, *Trivial Pursuit* is such a potentially useful model for classroom games that we will regard it as a paradigm in its own right. As every reader who has not just returned from a protracted stay on the Planet Zod is no doubt aware, the game involves moving round a circular track with radial connections to the FINISH circle in the centre, answering questions on different topics according to the colour of square landed on; the number of squares moved is determined by the throw of a die, but the direction of movement and the path taken at a junction are chosen by the player. The object of the game is to answer correctly one question on each topic and then end up on the FINISH circle, the first player to do so being the winner. Classroom games based on the *Trivial Pursuit* paradigm can be used to reinforce pupils' knowledge of virtually any topic in a way that they invariably find extremely enjoyable.

Illustrative example

A suggested skeleton model for a *Trivial Pursuit*-type game based on the general theme of the European Union (a topic that is taught at some stage in virtually all British schools) is shown in Figure 9.3. The board is a simplified version of the standard *Trivial Pursuit* board, but there are only four categories of questions as opposed to six in the original game. Although the four sets of questions can obviously be compiled by the teacher if this is thought appropriate, it is suggested that the overall educational value of the exercise will be greatly increased by getting the *pupils* to do this themselves, eg by asking each pupil to produce one question of each type. Readers who teach in British schools are invited to try developing such a game with their own pupils. Readers who teach in other countries can base it on their own local geography rather than on the European Union.

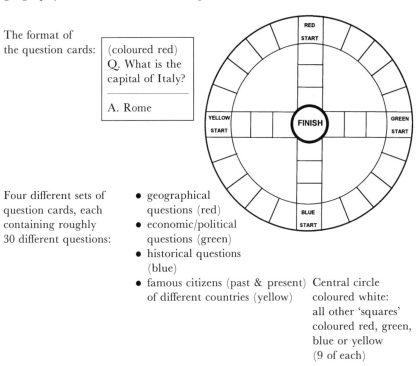

The format of the question cards:

| (coloured red) Q. What is the capital of Italy? |
| A. Rome |

Four different sets of question cards, each containing roughly 30 different questions:

- geographical questions (red)
- economic/political questions (green)
- historical questions (blue)
- famous citizens (past & present) of different countries (yellow)

Central circle coloured white: all other 'squares' coloured red, green, blue or yellow (9 of each)

Figure 9.3 A skeleton model for a *European Pursuit* game package.

Some useful paradigms for educational card games

Like board games, card games can take many different forms, but are nearly all based on a few standard underlying models. We will again take a look at some of the most important of these and see how they can be used for educational purposes.

The snap paradigm

This is an extremely simple model, and is based on the recognition of connections between cards, eg because they are identical, because they share a characteristic of some sort, or because they belong to a common set. The game is generally played by two players, each of whom is dealt half of the (shuffled) pack. The players take turns to place one of the cards face up on top of a common pile placed between them, and, when one of them recognizes a connection between the card that has just been laid down and the previous one, shouts 'Snap!' and claims the whole pile. The winner is the player who ends up with most cards, or still has cards left when play comes to an end. As we saw in Chapter 5, card games based on the *snap* paradigm are particularly useful in helping very young children to develop pre-maths and pre-reading skills of pattern-, shape- and colour-recognition. With slightly older children, they can be used to help them develop basic reading skills. With even older children, they can be used to reinforce teaching on sets and classifications.

Illustrative examples

The use of *snap*-type games to teach lower-primary pupils about their environment is discussed in detail in Chapter 5. This shows how a game based on the recognition of well-known flowers might be used with children of different ages. Another example of a possible *snap*-type game that could be used at both nursery and lower-primary levels is *Home Snap*. This might involve the use of a pack of, say, 48 cards, consisting of 12 sets of four cards that depict different things found in the home – a bed, a chair, a TV set, and so on. The objects shown on the cards could be varied by the teacher according to the age of the pupils and the particular aspect of home life that is being taught. The level of the game could also be varied by using three stepped packs – one with pictures only; one with pictures and names; one with names only.

The Happy Families paradigm

This is another extremely simple model, and is based on collecting sets of cards of the same type. The game is usually played by 3–5 players, to whom the entire pack of cards is dealt out. Players then try to collect complete sets of cards by asking one another if they have a particular card or set of cards, and, if they do, collecting it from them. The winner is the player that manages to collect most complete sets. With very young children, the 'sets' can simply be sets of identical cards, eg four 'dog' cards in a pack depicting different animals. With older children, the sets can be more complicated, with the cards in each set depicting different objects that have a common characteristic. Games based on the *Happy Families* paradigm can be used in much the same way as those based on the *snap* paradigm, eg for helping very young children to develop pre-maths and pre-reading skills, or for reinforcing the teaching of sets and classifications with older children. They also help children to develop their memory.

Illustrative examples

An example of a *Happy Families*-type game designed for use at lower-primary level – *Baking Happy Families* – is described in detail in Chapter 5 (see Figure 5.7). This is designed to reinforce the teaching of home economics, and also helps the children to develop their interpersonal and social skills. It involves collecting the various cards that make up recipes for baking different types of cakes and biscuits.

An example of a *Happy Families*-type game that can be used at upper-primary and lower-secondary levels is *Material Cards*. This is another of the exercises that was developed for use in teaching the 'Materials' section of the Scottish Foundation and General Level Science Curriculum. The composition of the pack of cards used in the game is shown in Figure 9.4, the players having to collect sets of the different types of materials. Note that the pack can also be used in games of the *snap*, *rummy* and *patience* type.

Set titles	Materials
Solid metals	gold, aluminium, copper, magnesium, lead, zinc
Rocks and minerals	diamond, quartz, coal, limestone, granite, slate
Man-made stony and ceramic materials	brick, concrete, tile, plaster, glass, porcelain
Plastics	nylon, polyurethane, cellophane, bakelite, perspex, vinyl
Solid plant products	wood, paper, cotton, rubber, hemp, cork
Solid animal products	wool, silk, fur, leather, horn, sponge
Liquids	water, glycerine, mercury, oil, petrol, sulphuric acid
Gases	oxygen, nitrogen, hydrogen, carbon dioxide, chlorine, methane

Figure 9.4 The composition of the *Material Cards* pack.

The rummy, poker *paradigm*

In games of this type, players are dealt a certain number of cards from which they have to try to compile matching sets or ordered sequences of some sort. In *rummy*, the member of the class that has by far the widest range of educational applications, players take turns to pick up and discard a single card, picking up their card either from the top of the inverted pack or from the top of the face-up pile of earlier discards. This enables them to improve their hands in a progressive manner, the winner being the first person to get rid of all their cards or compile the requisite number of sets or sequences. The great potential of this paradigm as a vehicle for helping to reinforce the teaching of matching, sets, patterns and classifications has been recognized since the earliest days of educational gaming.

Illustrative example

Games of the *rummy* type have proved particularly useful in the teaching of chemistry, since they are ideal for simulating the formation of chemical compounds from their constituent elements, ions and radicals. One of the classic examples is *Formulon*, a game published commercially by Chemistry Teaching Aids in 1973 for use in the lower-to-middle forms of secondary schools (see Figure 2.2). It is played in exactly the same way as ordinary rummy, the way in which cards can be used to build up scoring combinations or to change combinations already laid down being illustrated in Figure 9.5.

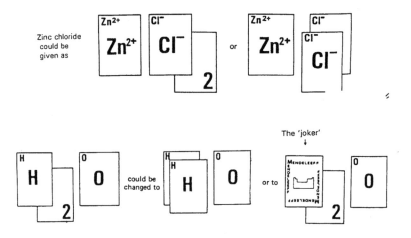

Figure 9.5 The way in which *Formulon* cards can be used to build chemical compounds.

The patience paradigm

This class of games includes all those where a single player tries to arrange a pack of cards in a particular way by going through a set procedure of some sort, thus trying to 'beat the system'. The *patience* principle can be used in a wide range of educational situations with pupils and students of all ages. It is particularly suitable for helping younger pupils to develop matching, classification and pattern-building skills, and for reinforcing the teaching of sets, classifications, relationships and transformations with older pupils and students. Educational games of this type have the further advantage that they can generally be played by small cooperative groups as well as by single players, thus fostering the development of team skills.

Illustrative example

Chemsyn is a highly sophisticated educational card game based on organic chemistry that was published by Heyden & Son Ltd in 1972. The game was designed for use in reinforcing knowledge of the properties of different types of organic compounds and of the transformations that can take place between them. The cards, which are themselves highly detailed 'revision cards' on the different compounds that they represent, can be used in various ways, eg in building up transformation patterns of the type shown in Figure 9.6. The game is designed for use both with senior pupils in secondary schools and with students at tertiary level.

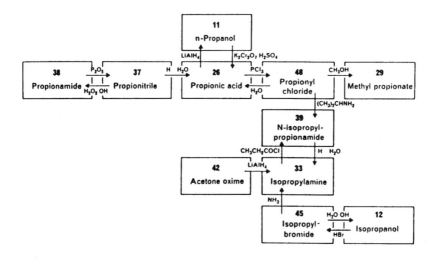

Figure 9.6 A typical *Chemsyn* transformation pattern.

The whist, bridge *paradigm*

This includes all games in which players are dealt hands of cards and then use these to win 'tricks' by deploying them in a certain way. Such games can be extremely sophisticated and demanding, and can be used to help pupils develop high-level cognitive skills relating to such things as tactical thinking and forward planning. They do not, however, lend themselves to the development of content-related educational games in the same way as the other basic paradigms described in this section. Indeed, the authors would be extremely interested to hear from any reader who can think of a way of relating a game based on this paradigm to a specific educational topic; *we* have not yet been able to do so!

Some other useful paradigms for educational games

Games can, of course, take a wide range of other forms apart from board and card games, and many of these are again well suited to adaptation for educational purposes. Some other useful paradigms for manual games will now be examined. (Readers interested in developing computer-based exercises should find all the paradigms they need among the various commercial packages now available.)

The crossword puzzle *paradigm*

It is assumed that all readers are familiar with this type of puzzle, which can be used to reinforce the teaching of virtually any topic by providing a vehicle whereby pupils and students can test their knowledge and understanding of the material covered. A typical example is shown in Figure 9.7. As can be seen, this is designed to test pupils' knowledge of astronomy. It was, incidentally, designed 'backwards', starting by thinking of possible answers to clues and fitting these together on a blank grid of squares, then blacking out the remaining squares to form the matrix for the puzzle, then producing the uncompleted version of the puzzle, and then (finally) writing the clues. This is much easier than working the other way round, and is an approach that is recommended to all aspiring writers of educational crossword puzzles. Note that the solutions to the puzzle shown in Figure 9.7 are given on p. 140, but readers may wish to try to solve it for themselves.

The lotto, bingo *paradigm*

Games of this type involve completing a card or matrix of some sort by collecting the items shown as they become available. The items to be collected

Astronomy Crossword

Across
1. Red giant in Orion's belt
3. The planet with the prominent rings
4. The wonderful star in the whale
5. The nearest star (think about this!)
6. The largest of 10 across
7. Bringer of war
8. Earth's cloud-covered sister planet
10. The remains of the former fifth planet?

Down
2. William Herschel discovered me in 1781
3. A monster of a moon
6. The largest moon of the largest planet
9. Also known as the Dog Star
11. Another red giant (in the Scorpion)

Figure 9.7 A typical educational crossword puzzle.

can be other (smaller) cards, tokens, symbols or numbers, with each player normally having to collect a different set; the winner is the first player to do so. The paradigm can be used for a wide range of educational purposes, particularly with younger children, with whom it can be used to develop pre-maths and pre-reading skills, to help them to develop basic reading skills, and to teach them about their environment.

Illustrative examples

The way in which lotto-type games can be used with very young children is discussed in Chapters 4 and 5. Chapter 4 describes a simple picture-lotto game that was developed by Monica Gordon in connection with her work on the 1990–91 Grampian Primary Industry Project at York Street Nursery School (see Figure 4.9). It was designed to reinforce the children's knowledge and recognition of things seen in and around Aberdeen harbour. Chapter 5 gives a detailed description of a stepped suite of listening-lotto games designed for use at lower-primary level (see Figure 5.1). These are designed to help the children develop their listening and reading skills.

Another simple lotto-type game that could be used both at nursery level and in the early forms of primary schools is *Animal Lotto*. In each case, the players would be provided with a 3 x 3 lotto card of the type shown in Figure 5.1, with the squares showing the pictures of different animals and each player's card containing a different sub-set of the set used in the game. (If it was decided to use 12 animals – six 'domestic' and six 'wild' – these might be: dog, cat, cow, sheep, pig, horse; lion, elephant, giraffe, monkey, kangaroo, crocodile.) In the nursery version of the game, a pack of 48 cards carrying exactly the same pictures would be shuffled and placed face down. The players would then take turns to pick up the top card, and, if it was one of those depicted on their own card, place it on the appropriate square. The winner would be the first player to collect all six. The lower-primary version of the game would be played in exactly the same way except that, in this case, the cards in the pack would carry the *names* of the different animals – either with or without the pictures, depending on the stage of development of the pupils.

The jigsaw paradigm

Games based on this paradigm involve fitting pieces together to produce a pattern or ordered whole. They are particularly suitable for use with very young children, with whom they can be used to develop pre-maths skills (matching, reinforcing relationships, etc) and psychomotor skills. They can also be used with older children to reinforce the teaching of patterns and relationships, eg of how different countries fit together to make up a continent such as Europe.

Illustrative examples

Several examples of educational games based on the jigsaw paradigm are described in Chapters 4 and 5. Both describe how linear jigsaws can be used to help very young children develop pre-maths, and pre-reading skills; see, for example, the *Rescue* linear jigsaw shown in Figure 4.4 and the 'walk in the park' linear jigsaw shown in Figure 5.2.

The use of 'two-dimensional' jigsaws is also described; see, for example, the stepped series of jigsaw patterns shown in Figure 4.5 and the description of the *Religions of the World* game given in Chapter 5. The latter involves completing a 'jigsaw' showing the parts of the world in which different religions are practised.

Other useful paradigms

Some other useful paradigms on which classroom games can be based include the dominoes paradigm and the dressing doll paradigm. The picture dominoes games described in Chapter 5 show how games based on the former can be used to help young children develop a wide range of skills; see, for example, the supermarket dominoes game shown in Figure 4.7, which is used to reinforce their experience of a visit to a supermarket. The use of dressing figure games with such children is also discussed in Chapter 4; see, for example, the *Dressing the Lifeboatman* game shown in Figure 4.6.

Some fundamental design principles

Readers who want to base an educational game on one of the above paradigms (or on any other paradigm that they think might be of use to them) should again bear the following fundamental design principles in mind.

- Make sure that the game has some clear *educational purpose*, preferably related to some specific aspect of the curriculum.
- Make sure that the *educational* and *gaming aspects* are properly integrated, so that the pupils cannot simply play it as a game without deriving any real educational benefit.
- Make sure that the *activities* and *materials* are appropriate to the age group for which the exercise is designed, eg by keeping them free of any dependence on number or written language if they are to be used with very young children who have not yet acquired basic number or reading skills.
- Design the package so that it can be *produced* in a reasonable time.
- Make sure that the exercise does not take *too long to play*.
- And, above all, make sure that it is *fun*!

Solutions to Astronomy Crossword

1a: Betelgeuse; 3a: Saturn; 4a: Mira; 5a: Sun; 6a: Eros; 7a: Mars; 8a: Venus; 10a: Asteroids; 2d: Uranus; 3d: Titan; 6d: Ganymede; 9d: Sirius; 11d: Antares.

10

Involving Pupils in the Design Process

Having looked in some detail at how teachers can set about designing games and simulations for use with their pupils, we will now end our book by showing how involving *the pupils themselves* in the design process can add a totally new dimension to the quality of their resulting educational experience.

The lessons learned from the Grampian Primary Industry Project

Throughout this book, extensive reference has been made to the 1990–91 Grampian Primary Industry Project, since a high proportion of the case-study material included in many of these chapters had its origins in this project, and all three of the authors were heavily involved in it. The project started in November 1990, when the official launch and a briefing conference for participating teachers were held in a Peterhead hotel (see Figure 2.3). It ended in May 1991, when it was brought to a climax with a public exhibition of the work carried out by the pupils and a debriefing conference for the teachers in Summerhill Education Centre, Aberdeen (see Figure 10.1). The project was organized by Bernard Brown, Grampian Region's Schools/Industry Liaison Officer, and Henry Ellington.

In between the Peterhead and Summerhill events, 32 classes in 25 primary schools (and one nursery school!) drawn from all parts of Grampian Region organized a wide range of individual projects designed to help the pupils learn about the 'business' side of industry. How they did this was up to the teachers, the only stipulation being that they had to make some use of games and simulations and form some sort of school–industry link.

The resulting class projects covered an extremely wide range of topics, eight being based on primary industries such as farming and oil, eight on

Figure 10.1 The Guest of Honour, Mr Graham Donaldson, HMCI (left) and Principal Sponsor Mr Richard Lawrence examining a board game developed by pupils of Anderson's Primary School, Forres at the Exhibition held at the end of the 1990–91 Grampian Primary Industry Project.

manufacturing industries such as biscuit-making and engineering, and 16 on service industries such as catering, tourism and the various branches of the media. All classes established at least one local industrial or commercial link, with over half establishing more than one – 13 in one case! All 32 classes also developed at least one classroom game or simulation for use in their projects, 17 making use of a whole-class, role-playing simulation of some sort, eg running a newspaper or business, 30 developing board games of various types, and eight developing other types of manual game such as card games. It is also interesting to note that none of the classes developed a computer game or simulation of any sort, although several made use of computers to support their projects, eg for word processing or desktop publishing, or to run commercial software packages relevant to their project themes.

The subsequent formal evaluation of the project (which was carried out by Henry Ellington on behalf of Grampian Education Authority) showed that it had been an outstanding success, and had fully achieved all its overall design aims. The evaluation also produced some extremely interesting information about how games and simulations had been used in the various class projects, and how effective they had been.

First, it confirmed that gaming and simulation techniques can be used extremely effectively at all levels of nursery and primary education, not only for reinforcing basic knowledge and understanding, but also for achieving high-level cognitive, affective and psychomotor objectives and developing a wide range of interpersonal, communication and other transferable-process skills. It also showed that such exercises can prove particularly effective when used *in combination*, eg by backing up a sophisticated role-playing simulation with complementary games of various types, as was done at Dales Park and Anderson's Primary Schools (see Chapter 6).

Second, it showed that teachers who have had little or no previous experience of designing or using classroom games or simulations can very quickly develop the necessary skills and confidence to do so if they are provided with basic initial guidance and subsequent encouragement and support. Of the 33 teachers who took part in the project, just over half had had some experience of using games and simulations, but very few had ever designed such exercises before. By the time the project was over, however, they were all fully competent in both areas, and many were planning to show their colleagues just how easy it all was!

Third, the evaluation showed that all but the very youngest pupils had played a major role in *designing* the games and simulations that had been developed in connection with their class projects (see Figure 10.2). Furthermore, it was clear that the pupils who had been actively involved in the design process had learned more from this experience than from actually *playing* the games and *participating* in the simulations. All the class teachers whose pupils had been so involved stressed the great educational benefits that they had derived from such work. These included the development of high-level cognitive and psychomotor skills (decision-making, problem-solving, graphic design and artistic skills), together with a wide range of communication, interpersonal and team skills. As would be expected, it was the more able pupils who tended to get most out of the design experience, but the less able also found it extremely worthwhile in most cases.

As a follow-up to the Grampian Primary Industry Project, Grampian Education Authority took active steps to promote the formation of school–industry links by *all* its schools, and to promote much wider use of classroom games and simulations. As we saw in the Introduction, one such measure was the development (by Joannie Fowlie and Henry Ellington) of a 'do-it-yourself' pack for teachers on the design and use of such exercises.

This stressed the additional educational benefits to be gained by actively involving pupils in the design process. The package was supplied to all nursery, primary and secondary schools in Grampian Region, and played a major role in encouraging teachers at all levels to make use of games and simulations with their classes – and to involve their pupils in the design of such exercises wherever possible. Let us now see how this was done in one particular school – Kincardine O'Neil Primary School in Aberdeenshire.

Figure 10.2 Pupils of Arduthie Primary School, Stonehaven, playing an educational game that they themselves devised; it involved answering questions as they moved round the 'board'.

Pupil involvement in game design: a detailed case study

Kincardine O'Neil Primary School is a small rural school 22 miles west of Aberdeen. It was one of the first schools to receive the 'do-it-yourself' package on games and simulations, which was given to six schools in different parts of Grampian Region prior to the main distribution in order to enable the authors of the package to carry out a summative evaluation of its effectiveness. The work carried out in Kincardine O'Neil Primary School was particularly closely monitored, with both Joannie Fowlie and Henry Ellington making regular visits to the school, and a video being made of the work carried out. This was later used for staff development purposes within Grampian Region, as well as being shown at a major international educational conference, where it aroused considerable interest.

At the time of the field trial of the package, Kincardine O'Neil Primary School had a total of 47 pupils divided into two composite classes – 22 in a P1–3 class and 25 in a P4–7 class. The teacher responsible for carrying out the trial was Mrs Linda Mudie, who taught the P4–7 class on two days a week in order to provide relief for the full-time teacher (Mrs Taylor) to carry out the administrative duties associated with her post as Head Teacher of the school. Mrs Taylor gave Mrs Mudie the package a few weeks before the end of the 1992 autumn term, and asked her to try it out with her pupils. Although she had no experience of using or designing classroom games, she readily agreed to do so.

Since Mrs Mudie had almost completed teaching her main theme for the term in question ('Farming'), she was unable to do very much about building the use of games into the mainline teaching of the topic. She did, however, ask the pupils to try to devise games based on the theme of 'Farming', dividing them into small groups for this work and providing them with general guidance based on the material in the package. She was sufficiently encouraged by the ease with which the pupils took to this work and by the educational benefits that resulted that she decided to build much of her teaching of the theme for the next term – 'Europe' – round the use of classroom games.

Mrs Mudie's work on 'Europe' was organized in a very systematic manner. She introduced the theme through a series of taught lessons, then left the pupils to carry out their own detailed research on the various aspects to be covered – the different countries of Europe, their languages, currencies, capitals, flags, etc, their geography, their main products, and so on. An extensive collection of resources was made available to them for this purpose. Mrs Mudie also divided her 25 pupils into five groups, asking each to devise a different game based on the information about Europe that they were steadily accumulating. Each group was given general guidelines about the type of game it should design, but it was left to them to decide on the exact form that it should take, to devise the rules, to produce all the playing materials, and to carry out the developmental trials. The five games that they eventually came up with were the following:

Game 1: Euro Card

This was a card game based on a combination of *Happy Families* and rummy. The pupils carried out detailed research on all 15 countries of the European Union, and produced a set of five cards on each, carrying different items of information. To play the game, each player (up to five) was dealt five cards; the remainder of the pack was then placed face down on the table between them, and the top card turned over and laid alongside it. Play then proceeded as in rummy, with each player picking up and discarding a single card on his or her turn. The winner was the first person to collect a full set of five cards on one particular country.

Game 2: Euro Bingo

This was based on the lotto/bingo principle. Each of up to four players had his or her own individual bingo card consisting of eight squares, each containing the *answer* to a particular question about Europe. There was also a question master, who had a pack of cards carrying the various questions on which the game was based (with the answers on the back), and worked through these in turn. If a player could recognize the answer to a question on their card, and had this confirmed by the question master, that particular square could be covered up. The winner was the first player to cover all eight squares.

Game 3: Spin a Disc

This was based on four sets of question cards, based on the capital cities, currencies, flags and languages of the different countries of Europe. These were placed in four envelopes, held by the question master. To play the game, players took turns to spin a pointer on a disc, the final position of which determined which category of question they should be asked by the question master. If they got the question right, they received a token. Each game lasted for exactly 10 minutes (timed by an electronic clock), at the end of which the winner was the player who had collected most tokens.

Game 4: Euro Beetle

This was based on the game beetle drive, a variation of lotto. Each player was given a lotto-type card for a different European country, with numbered spaces for six smaller cards showing its flag, currency, capital city, and so on. All these smaller cards were laid out on the centre of the table. To play, pupils took turns to throw a single die, collect the appropriate small card corresponding to the number shown (if they had not already done so), and place it on their large card. The winner was the first person to collect all six small cards on his or her country.

Game 5: Euro Trivial Pursuit

This was a board game based on *Trivial Pursuit* (and actually gave the authors the idea for the *European Pursuit* game described in Chapter 9 – see Figure 9.3). The board had three colours of square, corresponding to sets of questions on the languages, currencies and capital cities of the different European countries. There was also a fourth type of square which gave players an extra turn. Players took turns to throw a single die, moving by the number of squares shown and attempting to answer a question of the type indicated by the colour of the square on which they ended up (the sets of question cards were held by a question master). If they answered the question correctly, they collected a token, the winner being the first player to collect six tokens.

During the initial development phase of the project, each game was played mainly by the group responsible for designing it. Later, all the pupils in the class got a chance to play all the different games, so that the groups learned from one another's ideas, and also had the rules and playing procedures of their own games thoroughly field tested. This helped them to identify ways in which their games could be improved or the rules made more explicit.

From discussions with Mrs Mudie and her pupils, it was clear that, as in the Grampian Primary Industry Project, the children got a great deal more out of researching, designing and developing their games than they got out of subsequently playing the various games produced. The main benefits that they derived from the latter were reinforcement of their knowledge of the various countries of Europe and the development of basic communication, interpersonal and social skills. The research, design and development work, on the other hand, helped them to acquire skills of an altogether higher order. These included:

- the various skills associated with searching for, finding and interpreting information held in a variety of media
- problem-solving, decision-making, planning and evaluative skills
- the various written-language and 'legal' skills associated with writing the rules for their games
- a wide range of graphic, artistic and other psychomotor skills;
- a variety of IT skills
- high-level group and team skills.

Above all, it was clear that the pupils found the experience both enjoyable and highly motivating, making them keen to take on other demanding projects that would give them an opportunity to use their initiative and develop their creativity.

The authors hope that this account of the work carried out at Kincardine O'Neil, and the earlier accounts of similar work carried out in other Grampian schools, will encourage other teachers – at all levels of the education system – to try using games and simulations with their own classes. If it does, writing this book will have been well worthwhile!

Further Reading

Note that the various books included in this 'further reading' section are not listed in alphabetical order according to the name of the first author, as is conventional practice in academic texts. Rather, they have been listed in the order that the author of this book feels will be of greatest use to readers.

General books on educational gaming and simulation

Simulation/Games in Learning, Boocock, S S and Schild E O (1968) Sage Publications, Beverly Hills, CA. (One of the early classics – still worth reading, it contains the article by CC Not in which he gives his classic definition of a game – 'Games for Learning'.)

Simulation and Gaming in Education, Tansey, P J and Unwin, D (1969) Methuen, London. (Another early classic – also well worth reading.)

Learning and the Simulation Game, Taylor, J and Walford, R (1974) Open University Press, Milton Keynes. (Yet another early classic that is well worth reading.)

Gaming: The Future's Language, Duke, R D (1974) Wiley, New York. (Another extremely influential early classic.)

Principles and Practice of Gaming–Simulation, Greenblat C S and Duke, R D (1982) Sage Publications, Beverly Hills, CA. (Still one of the most useful general handbooks in the field.)

The Effective Use of Role Play: A Handbook for Teachers and Trainers, van Ments, M (1983) Kogan Page, London. (Another extremely useful general handbook.)

Simulations: A Handbook for Teachers and Trainers, Jones, K (1987) Kogan Page, London. (Yet another extremely useful general handbook.)

Gamester's Handbook: 140 Games for Teachers and Group Leaders, Brandes, D and

Phillips, H (1977) Hutchinson, London. (A rich sourcebook of short exercises for use in different situations.)

Gamesters' Handbook 2: More Games for Teachers and Group Leaders, Brandes, D (1982) Hutchinson, London. (A rich sourcebook of useful exercises.)

Icebreakers: A Sourcebook of Games, Exercises and Simulations, Jones, K (1992) Kogan Page, London. (Yet another rich sourcebook of useful exercises.)

Books dealing with the use of games in specific subject areas

Learning with Games, Charles, C L and Stadsklev R (eds) (1973) The Social Science Education Consortium Inc., Boulder, Colo. (An invaluable sourcebook on some of the most important early educational games and simulations in the field of social studies.)

Handbook of Simulation Gaming in Social Education, Stadsklev, R (1974) Institute of Higher Education Research and Services, University of Alabama, Birmingham, Ala. (Another invaluable sourcebook.)

Games and Social Life Skills, Bond, T (1986) Hutchinson, London. (An extremely useful sourcebook of short games in this area.)

Simulation in International Relations, Guetzkow, H (1963) Prentice-Hall, Englewood Cliffs, NJ.

Simulations in Language Teaching, Jones, K (1982) Cambridge University Press, Cambridge. (Another extremely useful sourcebook.)

Communication Games, Krupar, K R (1973) Macmillan, London. (Yet another extremely useful sourcebook.)

Games and Simulations in Science Education, Ellington, H I, Addinall, E and Percival, F (1981) Kogan Page, London. (The first book to deal specifically with science- and technology-based educational games – another useful sourcebook.)

Books on the design of games and simulations

A Handbook of Game Design, Ellington, H I, Addinall, E and Percival, F (1982) Kogan Page, London. (One of the first books dealing with the systems approach to game design.)

Case Studies in Game Design, Ellington, H I , Addinall, E and Percival, F (1984) Kogan Page, London. (The sequel to the 1982 *Handbook*, showing how the systems approach was applied to the design of 12 exercises of different types.)

Designing Your Own Simulations, Jones, K (1985) Methuen, London. (Another useful book on the design process.)

Designing Games and Simulations: An Illustrated Handbook, Greenblat, C (1988) Sage Publications, Newbury Park, CA. (One of the most comprehensive books yet written on game design.)

Designing and Evaluating Games and Simulations: A Process Approach, Gredler, M
(1992) Kogan Page, London. (Another extremely useful book for would-
be designers.)

A Guide to Games and Simulations as a Context for Learning, Fowlie, J and
Ellington, H (1992) Grampian Education Authority, Aberdeen. (The 'do-
it-yourself' pack for teachers issued to all Grampian Schools.)

Journals and Periodicals

Simulation and Games: An International Journal of Theory, Design and Research,
published quarterly by Sage Publications, Newbury Park, CA since 1970.
(The official journal of *ABSEL* (Association for Business Simulation and
Experiential Learning), *ISAGA* (International Simulation and Gaming
Association) and *NASAGA* (North American Simulation and Gaming
Association); an invaluable source of information on all aspects of
educational gaming and simulation.)

Simulation/Games for Learning (formerly *SAGSET Journal*) (The official journal
of the Society for Interactive Learning – formerly the Society for the
Advancement of Games and Simulations in Education and Training;
published quarterly from 1971–92; another invaluable source of information on all aspects of educational gaming and simulation.)

International Simulation and Gaming Yearbook, published annually by Kogan
Page, London since 1993. (This has replaced *Simulation/Games for Learning*
as the official publication of the Society for Interactive Learning; another
invaluable source of information on all aspects of educational gaming and
simulation.)

Information on Published Exercises

Many of the educational packages described in the main text have been published in some way. This section shows where these may be purchased, or where further information may be obtained.

Alternative Energy Project – a manual simulated case study on alternative energy; developed by H Ellington and E Addinall; published by Association for Science Education, College Lane, Hatfield, Herts. AL10 9AA in 1980; price £10.

Amsyn Problem – a manual simulation/game based on chemical engineering; developed by F Percival and N Reid; published by Scottish Council for Educational Technology, Dowanhill, Victoria Crescent Road, Glasgow in 1976.

Bert Boot – a stepped suite of computer games on basic multiplication and division; published by HS Software; price £6.95 (cassette), £7.95 (disc).

Bruce Oil Management Game – a computer-based simulation/game centred on the North Sea oil industry that was used as the basis of a national (later international) competition between 1974–75 and 1979–80, and also as an exercise for students; further information available from School of Computer and Mathematical Sciences, The Robert Gordon University, Aberdeen.

Carry Add – a stepped suite of computer games on basic addition and subtraction; published by HS Software; price £6.95 (cassette), £9.95 (disc).

Chemsyn – an organic chemistry-based card game; published by Heyden & Son Ltd., Spectrum House, Hillview Gardens, London NW4 2JQ in 1972.

Contract 3-5 – a board game based on business contracts; developed by J Fowlie; described in detail in *A Guide to Games and Simulations as a Context for Learning* (see Further Reading).

Culraggie Whisky Game – a board game based on the whisky industry;

developed by H Edge; described in detail in *A Guide to Games and Simulations as a Context for Learning* (see Further Reading).

Damascus Reporter – a computer simulation based on the life of St Paul; developed by G Bagnall; published by Appian Way Software, Durham; price £12.50.

Dressing the Lifeboatman – a manual game developed by M Gordon; described in detail in *A Guide to Games and Simulations as a Context for Learning* (see Further Reading).

Ekofisk – One of a Kind – a package of manual games, simulations and case studies on the North Sea oil and gas industry; developed by H Ellington and E Addinall; published by Phillips Petroleum in 1980 as part of their multimedia educational library of the same name; further information available from Phillips Petroleum Public Affairs Department, London.

Firefight – a computer game designed to develop basic reading skills; published by HS Software as part of *Reading Pack 1* (see opposite).

Formulon – a chemistry-based card game; published by Chemistry Teaching Aids, Letham, Ladybank, Fife KY7 7RN in 1973.

Health Snakes and Ladders – a board game developed by H Ellington and E Addinall; published by Scottish Curriculum Development Service, Dundee Centre, Northern College, Dundee DD5 1NY in 1984.

Lebensraum – a board game based on competition by rival species for territory; developed by H Ellington and E Addinall; published by Scottish Curriculum Development Service, Dundee Centre, Northern College, Dundee DD5 1NY in 1984.

Letterbugs – a computer game for developing advanced reading skills; published by HS Software as part of *Reading Pack 4* (see below).

Licensed to Drill – a package of manual and computer games, simulations and case studies based on the economics of the North Sea oil industry; developed by H Ellington and E Addinall; published by Phillips Petroleum in 1985 as part of their multimedia educational library of the same name; further information available from Phillips Petroleum Public Affairs Department, London.

Material Cards – a suite of card games based on classification of materials; developed by H Ellington and E Addinall; published by Scottish Curriculum Development Service, Dundee Centre, Northern College, Dundee DD5 1NY in 1984.

Maths Pack 1 – a stepped series of computer games designed to develop basic number skills; published by HS Software; price £12.95 (disc).

Microbe Attack – a board game based on microbe infection; developed by H Ellington and E Addinall; originally published under name *Virus Attack* by Scottish Curriculum Development Service, Dundee Centre, Northern College, Dundee DD5 1NY in 1984.

North Sea Auction – a simulation/game based on the North Sea oil industry; originally published as part of *Licensed to Drill* package (see opposite).

Power for Elaskay – a manual simulation exercise based on alternative energy; developed by H Ellington and E Addinall; published by the Institution of Electrical Engineers Schools Liaison Service, Michael Faraday House, Stevenage SG1 2AY in 1978.

Power for Pemang – a revised version of *Power for Elaskay*; published by the IEE's Schools Liaison Service in 1994.

Reading Pack 1 – a stepped suite of computer games designed to develop basic reading skills; published by HS Software; price £9.95 (cassette), £12.95–£14.95 (disc).

Reading Pack 4 – a stepped suite of computer games designed to develop advanced reading skills; published by HS Software; price £9.55 (cassette), £12.95 (disc).

Rescue – a manual game based on rescue at sea; developed by M Gordon; described in detail in *A Guide to Games and Simulations as a Context for Learning* (see Further Reading).

Sortout – a computer game designed to develop advanced reading skills; published by HS Software as part of *Reading Pack 4* (see above).

Splashdown – a computer game designed to develop basic reading skills; published by HS Software as part of *Reading Pack 1* (see above).

Starpower – a manual simulation/game based on the stratification and conflict that invariably develop in an unregulated free-market society; published by Simile 11, 1150 Silverado Street, La Jolla, CA 92037 in 1969.

Survival – a manual game based on the predator–prey relationship; developed by H Ellington and E Addinall; published by Scottish Curriculum Development Service, Dundee Centre, Northern College, Dundee DD5 1NY in 1984.

WFF'N Proof – a suite of manual games based on symbolic logic; developed by L Allen; published by Autotelic Instructional Materials Publishers, New Haven, Conn. in 1962.

Which Material? – a manual case study based on the selection of materials for making different artefacts; developed by H Ellington and E Addinall; published by Scottish Curriculum Development Service, Dundee Centre, Northern College, Dundee DD5 1NY in 1984.

Index

Where a topic has been dealt with in depth, **bold type** indicates the page(s) where discussion of the topic begins. Note that the names of specific games or simulations are given in *italics*.